Minnesota State Parks
Celebrating One Hundred Years

Common Loon (Gavia immer) (Paul Sundberg)

Mike Link and Kate Crowley

Voyageur Press

Acknowledgments

Minnesota's state parks have been part of many experiences for my wife Kate and me; they have been a source of pleasures that we would like to share with you.

We appreciate the Minnesota Department of Natural Resources for its foresight and good management of the parks. There is a delicate balance between protecting the resource and providing recreation.

The park managers, regional managers and naturalists, and staff in the St. Paul office have given this material their review and critique, and that has helped shape the text.

For Kate and me, writing this book has deepened our love and fascination for the state. This collection of essays on the geology, biology, and history of the areas has given us a real sense of place and a greater respect for Minnesota.

Printed in Hong Kong
90 91 92 93 94   5 4 3 2 1

Library of Congress Cataloging-in-Publication Data

Link, Michael.
    Minnesota State Parks; celebrating one hundred years/Mike Link.
      p. cm.
    ISBN 0-89658-103-9
      1. Minnesota — Description and travel — 1891 — Guide-books.
    2. Parks — Minnesota — Guide-books. I. Title.
    F604.3.L56 1990
    917.7604'53 — dc20   89-77801
                                                                          CIP

Jacket and book design by Lou Gordon

Published by Voyageur Press, Inc.
P.O. Box 338
123 North Second Street
Stillwater, MN 55082 U.S.A.
In Minn 612-430-2210
Toll-free 800-888-9653

Voyageur Press books are also available at discounts for quantities for educational, fundraising, premium, or sales-promotion use. For details contact the marketing manager. Please write or call for our free catalog of natural history publications.

CONTENTS

INTRODUCTION

The Minnesota State Park system celebrates its one hundredth anniversary in 1991. The occasion marks the establishment of Itasca State Park on April 20, 1891. Today, there are sixty-five state parks located throughout the state, preserving some of Minnesota's most outstanding natural and cultural resources. The state parks are also renowned for their scenic beauty and a wealth of recreational opportunities.

This book has been compiled to give readers an overview of the current state park system. It includes information on the plants, animals, history, geology, and recreational opportunities that are found in each park. While a book of this size cannot be comprehensive, it is hoped that the reader will gain a sense of what is unique about each park, and what incredible diversity the state park system makes available.

Chapters are arranged by grouping parks according to a common feature, although some parks could easily fall into several categories. There are forest parks, prairie parks, lake parks, and parks with historic sites. Parks along the North Shore of Lake Superior, the Mississippi River, the St. Croix River, and the Minnesota River have been clustered into chapters. To help readers easily locate specific parks, an alphabetical listing is in the back of the book.

Ten parks have been highlighted as *major parks*, and ten have been highlighted as *hidden gems*. Major parks, as the name implies, tend to be the busiest parks, with many facilities and large summertime crowds. Hidden gems, on the other hand, are parks with many special features, but for one reason or another, they have not been "discovered" by most people. These hidden gems contain some of the finest natural and cultural resources in the park system. If you have never been to any of the hidden gems, they are all worth a trip!

For one hundred years, Minnesotans and out-of-state visitors have enjoyed vacationing at Itasca State Park, site of the famous headwaters of the Mississippi River. Through the years, many other parks have become popular, and state parks are now used extensively during all seasons. With wise stewardship and your support, the Minnesota State Park system will continue to be one of the nation's premier park networks for many generations to come.

For more terrific information about Minnesota's state parks, contact the Department of Natural Resources Information Center:

DNR Information Center
500 Lafayette Road
St. Paul, MN 55155–4040
Twin Cities: 296–4776
Toll-free in Minnesota: 800–652–9747 (ask for DNR)
Telecommunications device for deaf: 612–296–5484

Cover photographs: Lac qui Parle sunrise (Walt Huss), Bear Head Lake State Park (Greg L. Ryan and Sally A. Beyer), Mississippi headwaters (Greg L. Ryan and Sally A. Beyer), Split Rock Lighthouse (Paul Sundberg), Cascade River (Paul Sundberg), and Loons (Peter Roberts).

HISTORY OF MINNESOTA'S STATE PARKS

The natural beauty of Minnesota was recognized very early in the development of the territory, even before Minnesota became a state. In 1835, artist George Catlin visited Fort Snelling and spent considerable time sketching the Dakota Indians who lived around the fort and in southwestern Minnesota. Catlin was popular out east for his painting of Native Americans, and his influence extended beyond his paintbrush. The eastern press was anxious to publish Catlin's accounts of this frontier territory, especially accounts that implored travelers to change their plans and make their next fashionable tour up the Mississippi to the "thousand bluffs which tower in majesty above the river." He was writing about the Minnehaha Falls area.

In 1836, Nathan Jarvis wrote of Minnehaha Falls and the area around Fort Snelling: "I should not be surprised that in a few years this place will be as great as Niagara." In the fifty-five years that separated the writing of these words and the start of the park system, the very appearance and make-up of the area changed drastically. The surrounding territory became a state, and Minneapolis and St. Paul became the metropolitan centers of Minnesota. Beavers were trapped nearly to extinction, the fur trade was reduced to a minor portion of the state economy, the Dakota Indians were defeated by the Ojibwe and then by the military, transportation was reshaped by the railroads, and white pine loggers had started to cut forests throughout the northeast region.

The movement to establish a park system in Minnesota began as early as 1875, with an effort to designate the Minnehaha Falls area as a state park. In 1885, the legislature authorized a commission to select and locate "certain lands in the county of Hennepin" for a state park. A governor's committee was appointed. The landscape architect H. W. S. Cleveland, who eventually became a Minneapolis park commissioner, made a strong plea for Minnehaha Falls as a state park, stating, "It [Minnehaha Falls] is liable, however, at any time to be ruthlessly destroyed, and some of its features have already been defiled by being made receptacles of all the rubbish and filth of the adjacent beer gardens." In 1889, Camp Release State Memorial Wayside was established. This parkland was eventually turned over to the state's historical society.

Then in 1891, the legislature established Itasca State Park. Supervision of the park was under the state auditor, who also acted as land commissioner. The law prohibited the willful cutting, destroying, or mutilating of "any tree, timber or evergreen." The law also made it illegal to "kill or cause to be killed any moose, bear, deer, fox, otter or any other wild animal." The legislation to establish Itasca was the result of efforts by Jacob Brower, the surveyor, archaeologist, county auditor, seaman, cavalryman, state representative, lawyer, and explorer who mapped the Lake Itasca area and ended the controversy over the true headwaters of the Mississippi. The effort to pass the legislation was not without opposition, and even after passage there was no money for acquisition. Itasca was just a park on paper.

Brower became the first park commissioner for Itasca State Park. Until his death in 1905, he fought for acquisition of Itasca's lands while fighting against poachers, politicians, and lumbermen. He wrote, "No one will ever realize how necessarily strenuous were the exertions which finally resulted in establishing Itasca State Park. . . ." Today we recognize Jacob Brower as the founder of Itasca State Park and the father of the Minnesota State Park system.

The next park came with the authorization to create the Dalles of the St. Croix Park in 1895, now called Interstate State Park. The park was established simultaneously with its Wisconsin counterpart, the first time a two-state cooperative park had been achieved.

Minneopa State Park was added in 1905 after grasshopper plagues caused Minneopa Village to be abandoned. Fort Ridgely in 1911, Jay Cooke in 1915, Whitewater in 1919, Sibley in 1919, Scenic in 1921, Lake Bemidji in 1923, and Lindbergh in 1931 complete the list of the first ten state parks. U. W. "Judge" Hella, director of the park system from 1951 to 1973, once stated that "All state parks are born in bitterness." The battles are usually long and harsh, but after they are over the parks represent our most cherished possessions.

Administration of the parks, waysides, and monuments was scattered among various state agencies, and in 1935, the Division of Parks (now part of the Department of Natural Resources) was established to take control. In 1937, thirteen new parks were added to more than double the size of the system. This was followed by a comprehensive state park plan in 1938. The plan's goal was to create a park or recreation area within thirty miles of every state resident. While that goal has not been reached, over seven million visitors have used Minnesota's state parks, and in 1988, four out of five of the visitors were Minnesotans.

* * *

The history, variety, and beauty of the Minnesota landscape are now part of a hundred years of state park history. This centennial celebration is a good time to reflect on the quality of our park system. There are sixty-five parks within the state, and they are scattered across the map. The state park system also continues to administer fourteen wayside rests around the state.

Over two hundred thousand acres were selected to preserve our state's beauty and to protect rare and sensitive plants, animals, land forms, and historic resources. Our parks protect the landscape and the history of Minnesota from overdevelopment, as well as misuse. A hundred years ago, the demand was based on fewer users and few options for recreation. Today, the park system's decisions must balance protection of the resource and opportunity for the visitor.

And the opportunities seem endless. The trails offer hiking, backpacking, cross-country skiing, skate skiing, snowmobiling, bicycling, and horseback riding. Boaters canoe and kayak, sail and water-ski. All kinds of campers enjoy the parks: small groups or organized group campers; canoers; backpackers; horseback riders; and visitors who walk in, cart in, or drive in with tents or motorized campers. There are picnic shelters and beaches. The park system manages a lodge, a chalet, cabins, and ten modern group centers with cabins. Still, there is demand for more. Each new invention for recreation creates new users and more pressure on park resources.

On top of management of people, facilities, recreation, and roadways, the park system is responsible for the natural environment. In the parks today, there are numerous prairie restoration projects and some forest management demonstration areas. Endangered species are monitored and special efforts like the re-establishment of peregrine falcons are part of the park program. Education through interpretation is a significant part of the park experience, and there are many visitor centers to help explain the parks' natural and cultural histories. In many parks, the visitor center is part of the local school program, and area residents join campers for the naturalists' presentations. Nature trails with information posted on signs or with instructional booklets, called self-guided trails, have been part of the park experience for years. And now kiosks and graphics present additional information. In the 1930s and 1940s, the Works Projects Administration (WPA) and the Civilian Conservation Corps (CCC) cleared trails, built structures, and gave visitors access to the parks' resources. Many of their projects are now historic monuments themselves, classic examples of rustic architecture.

The views of park visitors were expressed in a 1987 survey. Over 80 percent of the users surveyed felt that a state park should include picnic areas, hiking trails, campgrounds, visitor centers, showers, and beaches. And the majority felt that amusement rides, motorized off-road vehicle trails, hunting, golf courses, and motels or lodges were not appropriate. It was the natural experience of beautiful scenery, peace, quiet, and nature, combined with fun and exercise that had the most appeal.

Park Director Bill Morrissey wrote, "One of the foremost purposes of the Minnesota State Park system is environmental education. Our 65 state parks serve as outdoor laboratories for enjoyment and education. . . ." Judge Hella summed up the park purpose when he wrote, " . . . each of our parks is designed to hold the unique character of a region: its vegetation, its soil, its animal life, its rocks and waters, its legends and lore."

THE FOREST PARKS

Minnesota's state park visitors have a choice between the dense conifer forest, with its carpet of needles, and the more open deciduous forests, with a rich green garden of ferns and flowers. The coniferous forests include the Great Lakes pine forest and the southern edge of the boreal forest, which reaches into Canada. The Great Lakes pine forest is dominated by conifers—pines in the uplands and black spruce and tamarack in the peatlands. Bear Head Lake, George Crosby Manitou, McCarthy Beach, Scenic, Schoolcraft, Lake Bemidji, and Itasca state parks are part of this pineland complex. There are pinelands on central Minnesota's sand plains too. And red and jack pine are mixed with the prairie ground cover in St. Croix State Park near Hinckley and Hayes Lake State Park in the northwest corner of Minnesota.

Some of the state's hardwood forests are remnants of the Big Woods, a maple-basswood complex that once dominated the glacial moraine region from St. Cloud to Minneapolis. Nerstrand Big Woods, Lake Maria, and Sakatah Lake state parks fall into this category. The deciduous forest becomes more diverse toward the southern edge of Minnesota, where Beaver Creek Valley, Flandrau, and Forestville state parks are located. Valuable black walnut, hickory, and black cherry are abundant in this region. The driftless area of southeastern Minnesota, where the most recent glaciers did not reach, has well-mixed woods; the area may have been a natural nursery for reforesting the state after the glaciers left.

Oaks grow on prairies in habitat known as oak savannas. Bur oaks are the dominant trees in locations such as Kilen Woods State Park. Extensive flood plain forests are well developed along the Mississippi and Minnesota rivers. Frontenac, Lac qui Parle, and Minnesota Valley state parks contain good examples of flood plain forests.

Beaver Creek Valley State Park (Bob Firth)

Nestled in the blufflands in southeastern Minnesota, Beaver Creek Valley State Park is in a deep wooded valley in the midst of farmland. Here, the most recent glacial ice did not cover the landscape, but meltwater from the ice sheets did flow over the land and extended the glacial sculpturing in the valley. The waters rushed across ancient beds of dolomite and sandstone, flat layers of sedimentary rock that were deposited in seabeds 500 to 430 million years ago, and deepened streambeds into valleys. Over the centuries, more water has deepened these valleys as it flows to the Mississippi River. The result of all this stream erosion is a pattern of bluffs and valleys.

In Beaver Creek Valley water has eroded through the Oneota dolomite and Jordan sandstone, opening up the ground to the flowing groundwater within the bedrock. The result is a spring that is the origin of almost the entire flow of Beaver Creek. The stream's cold waters support a native brook trout population, as well as brown trout. These brookies reach trophy size and are a good challenge to fly-fishing anglers.

A forest of willow, box elder, cottonwood, and elm fills the valley, while a mix of maple, walnut, basswood, and oak climbs the slopes. In the springtime, early blooming wildflowers fill the woodland hills and valleys. All summer long, the combination of shade and the cold water stream keeps this valley cooler than the surrounding tableland.

The creek is a draw to both humans and wildlife. American redstarts, song sparrows, cedar waxwings, woodpeckers, and a variety of flycatchers can be found along the stream and in the woods. The Acadian flycatcher, a rare bird in Minnesota, is seen in this valley — the only place it is regularly reported. The Louisiana water thrush also nests here. Wild turkeys and ruffed grouse can be heard in the spring.

A swinging bridge crosses the stream to a picnic shelter with a small visitor center. The park also has modern tent, group, and walk-in campsites, and ski and hiking trails. On the north end of the park is the privately owned Schech's Mill. Built in 1875 to 1876, this mill represents "The New Process" era of milling that sprung up around 1871 to 1880. The mill is still operating and is open for tours.

The north end of the valley is broader. Farmland abuts the stream and the land rolls gently away. Hiking trails have excellent vistas for those who like exercise and quiet. The playground and children's wading pool entertain the kids. Families can sit in natural coolness on hot summer days or return in the fall when the hardwood forests put on a colorful display.

For more information about this park contact: Beaver Creek Valley State Park, Route 2, Box 57, Caledonia, MN 55921. Phone 507–724–2107. See also the address for the DNR Information Center at the front of the book.

Beaver Creek Valley State Park (Minnesota DNR)

Dutchman's Breeches (Dicentra cucullaria) (Joe Niznik)

Camden meets all the criteria for being one of Minnesota's hidden gems. Visitors find that the entrance road quickly plunges out of sight of the highway. From the prairie grasses and forbs, the road descends through a hardwood forest into a narrow river valley and crosses the cold, clear Redwood River.

Woods, marsh, and prairie mix in this southwestern park, but the woodlands dominate. A complex of maple, basswood, oak, and cottonwood trees is sorted by the direction and angle of the slopes, the stream bottomlands, and the blufftops. Clear water bubbles from springs, keeping the Redwood River crystal clear and open all year for trout. In these surroundings, anglers cast for brown trout, and picnickers escape the prairie heat and listen to the stream's music. Downstream, a cold water impoundment is a swimming pool, where kids romp on hot days.

The river that flows through the park, the Redwood, is named for the red osier dogwood that grows along the banks on the slower portions of the river's route. The river flows north from the Coteau des Prairies, the "highland of the prairies" region, then drops 100 to 150 feet during its two-mile journey through Camden State Park, and continues across the lowland plains to a junction with the Minnesota River. From Sioux Lookout, visitors can survey the Redwood River lowlands all the way to Marshall.

The Redwood River was the site of an American Fur Company post. Joseph La Framboise operated the post until he was lured away by George Catlin, the great painter of Native Americans, to serve as a guide and interpreter. The stream provided good drinking water and harbored fur bearers, but it also attracted elk, bison, deer, and pronghorn. Today, campers, hikers, cross-country skiers, and anglers have taken the place of the natives and the fur trader. The white-tailed deer is the only big game animal left.

In a region that is among the least wooded in the state, this forest is special. All three species of Minnesota squirrel live in these woods — the red, gray, and fox. In the spring only a few flowers color the grasslands, but the deciduous woods are a royal garden. In the prairie, the grasses glow warm orange each autumn, and the hardwood forest is ablaze with color.

The park is named for the old city of Camden, Minnesota. Near the village the Jones Gristmill operated with no competition for fifty miles. Other settlers came to the valley from 1868 to 1888 to build a general store, hotel, blacksmith shop, and sawmill. By 1930, there was nothing left of the town. The old townsite and Camden Woods became a favorite picnic site for residents of the area. Mink and raccoons returned, trilliums and jewelweeds re-established themselves, and bluebirds perched on the prairie shrubs.

Camden State Park features a small visitor center and a warming house. The park has two picnic areas, two modern campgrounds, a horse-back campground, and a group campground. Trails for hikers, skiers, horses, snowmobiles, and bikes sample the natural diversity and the varied terrain. Along Indian Creek trail are featured quotes from Sigurd Olson's *Hidden Forest*, encouraging contemplation. Brawner Lake Wildlife Management Area has been added to the park, and provides bass and bluegill fishing, canoeing, and swimming. An additional specialty of the park is the annual wildlife art exhibit, which spotlights prominent wildlife artists each August.

For more information about this park contact: Camden State Park, Route 1, Box 9, Lynd, MN 56157. Phone 507-865-4530. See also the address for the DNR Information Center at the front of the book.

Camden State Park (Bill Rooks)

Jack-in-the-Pulpit (Arisaema triphyllum) (Joe Niznik)

Redwood River, Camden State Park (Marlin Meyer)

FRANZ JEVNE

This small northern park protects a portion of the Rainy River shoreline and provides a river campsite for paddlers who are going from Voyageur National Park, Big Fork River, or Little Fork River to Lake of the Woods.

This is rustic; the sounds and the scenes are peaceful. A gravel road leads off Highway 11 to a boat access on the Rainy River. From there, a rougher road leads to a picnic and small camping area. A minimum number of amenities are hewn out of the forest, including a pit toilet, a pump, and sixteen campsites with tables. The picnic area is a small walk-in site on the banks of the Sault Rapids. Across the river is Canada.

One hiking trail leads out of the campground, and short paths provide access to the river for fishing. Walleye, northerns, smallmouth bass, and sturgeon are in the river.

The woods are undisturbed and summer visitors can see the colorful fruit of red and white baneberry and blue cohosh, as well as the flowers of skullcap and fringed loosestrife, which is part of the primrose family.

For more information about this park contact: Franz Jevne State Park, Route 3, Box 230, Birchdale, MN 56629. No Phone. See also the address for the DNR Information Center at the front of the book.

Franz Jevne State Park
(Carmelita McGurk/Minnesota DNR)

14

GEORGE H. CROSBY MANITOU

This is back country. There are no flush toilets and wells. Here, park users have a wilderness of fir, cedar, spruce, and northern hardwoods to explore. Beautiful old-growth stands are protected as part of a Scientific and Natural Area.

The Manitou River plunges through a volcanic canyon with eight major waterfalls in the last seven miles (most on private property). The last waterfall drops almost directly into Lake Superior. The river drains a large area outside the park that includes eleven small lakes and ten square miles of alder, tamarack, and cedar swamps. These tannin-stained waters have a more reliable flow than some other North Shore rivers.

There is one easy hiking trail around Benson Lake, but most of the trails are rugged with steep grades. Even at the isolated campsites along the lake or the river, campers should take the precaution of treating the water before drinking it. There are brook trout and splake in the lake, and many kinds of trout in the river—brown, rainbow, and brook.

This park is rugged and exciting. Moose, deer, bears, and wolves share the trails with hikers. Only the woodland caribou is missing from the original fauna of the park. In the winter the animals' tracks cross the ski and snowshoe trails. Ski trails are not groomed and skiers need to be intermediate to expert in skill.

For more information about this park contact: Information available from Tettegouche State Park, 474 Highway 61 E., Silver Bay, MN 55614. Phone 218–226–3539. See also the address for the DNR Information Center at the front of the book.

Manitou River, George H. Crosby Manitou State Park (Bob Firth)

KILEN WOODS

Ravines. Kilen Woods is a complex of ravines and intermittent streams in wooded and grassy valleys that lead to the Des Moines River. Glaciers shaped the landscape here. The Des Moines River, a dominant feature in the park, flows through an old glacial meltwater channel.

Trails meander down the hillsides under the shade of the oak forests, cross the flood plain, and continue on to the prairie. Rose-breasted grosbeaks, vireos, and scarlet tanagers call in the woods. Kingfishers, herons, and song sparrows patrol the river's edge; bluebirds, wood ducks, and tree swallows nest in various cavities and boxes.

Beaver and muskrat use the river. White-tailed deer, squirrels, blue jays, and wood ducks feed on the abundant acorn crop. Red admiral butterflies, fritillaries, thirteen-lined ground squirrels, and rare grasshopper mice feed in the prairies.

There are two prairie areas in the park. The tall grass prairie, with its beautiful display of gray coneflowers, butterfly weed, and grasses as tall as seven feet, is joined by hill prairies in Kilen Woods. Oaks mix with shorter grassland plants on the hillsides. This hillside habitat hosts the largest population of the rare prairie bush clover in the state.

The park offers camping, canoeing, picnicking, and hiking; in the winter the most daring can swoosh down the long, steep tubing hill.

For more information about this park contact: Kilen Woods State Park, Route 1, Box 122, Lakefield, MN 56150. Phone 507–662–6258. See also the address for the DNR Information Center at the front of the book.

Kilen Woods State Park (Bill Rooks)

Lake Louise State Park is less than two miles from Highway 56, but the park becomes obvious long before its sign does. In the middle of pasture and cropland is a serene oak savanna.

A thin veneer of glacial soil covers the limestone bedrock. Lake Louise has no hills, only occasional depressions where ground water has eroded and dissolved the rock and formed small sink holes.

The lush soils that support a farm economy also support a luxurious carpet of spring flowers. The rare nodding wild onion grows here and nowhere else in Minnesota.

This natural oasis also supports wildlife, including fox squirrels, raccoons, red foxes, and white-tailed deer. Turtles lounge along the river banks and sun themselves on tree trunks that have tumbled into the lake.

Two rivers converge here, the Little Iowa and the Upper Iowa. Lake Louise, actually an impoundment, was formed by the gristmill dam built by the Hambrecht family and the original community of LeRoy. When the railroad came, LeRoy moved south to meet it. The Hambrechts donated the millpond and surrounding land to the village of LeRoy, and it became known as Wildwood Park. In 1962, LeRoy donated the park to the Department of Natural Resources. The park became the heart of the present-day 1,168-acre state park.

Today the local citizens still swim and picnic here, and tourists come to birdwatch, canoe, ride horses, hike, camp, and cross-country ski. The park provides trails for snowmobiling and contains a small historical facility housed in the Hambrecht's old summer cabin.

For more information about this park contact: Lake Louise State Park, Route 1, Box 184, LeRoy, MN 55951. Phone 507–324–5249. See also the address for the DNR Information Center at the front of the book.

Monarch Butterfly (Danus plexippus) on Beggar's-Ticks (Bidens sp.) (Connie Wanner)

LAKE MARIA

Forest covers the steep hills of Lake Maria State Park, reminiscent of the Big Woods, a complex of maple, basswood, and other deciduous trees. The rugged terrain is the result of glacial moraine deposits from the St. Croix Moraine.

The forest is dense and trees march over the roadway in search of sun. In autumn, the maples turn brilliant hues of red and orange. The lakes and ponds are small and provide fishing for northerns, walleye, bass, and panfish. The lakes are also good for canoers, and an assortment of waterfowl makes the lakes popular with birdwatchers.

Backpackers and primitive-style campers can find campsites to suit their needs, and the trail network is designed for both hikers and horseback riders. A trail center provides educational displays and a winter warming house.

In the winter, Lake Maria State Park becomes very special. The steep woodland trails provide cross-country skiers with variety, excitement, and solitude. Wildlife tracks mark the snow, winter birds sit in the branches, and winter campers find the backcountry free from crowds, insects, and heat.

Located close to the Twin Cities, this park is perfect for one- and two-day excursions.

For more information about this park contact: Lake Maria State Park, Route 1, Box 128, Monticello, MN 55362. Phone 612-878-2325. See also the address for the DNR Information Center at the front of the book.

*White Water Lily (*Nymphaea odorata*)*
(Greg L. Ryan and Sally A. Beyer)

NERSTRAND BIG WOODS

Among the few remnant areas of Minnesota's Big Woods, Nerstrand Big Woods is the biggest. While other areas protect plant samples, this state park offers the best opportunity for the full biological community to exist and be explored.

Naturalists use the term "Big Woods" to represent an area of hardwood forest of maples and basswood that once dominated south central Minnesota. Maple and basswood trees, once they have become established, have the ability to reproduce and replace themselves. The seedlings of the maple can grow in the shade of the understory; therefore, the old maple may be replaced by its offspring. The basswood will establish shoots from the base of the older tree when wind, disease, or other natural causes remove the mature tree. For these reasons, the Big Woods became a very stable forest—until the axe and saw were introduced.

Nerstrand Big Woods is a floral garden; it is a photographer's, a naturalist's, and a hiker's delight. Rich humus lines the forest floor. The warmth of the spring sunshine is collected by last year's brown leaves. Naked branches wave in the April winds and the buds swell as sap moves up the trunk. The springtime forest floor is a mesh of shadows and sunlight.

In the spring many plants grow quickly, flower, produce seeds, and become dormant in the short time between the melt of the snow and the full shade of summer. These plants are known as spring ephemerals. Sharp-lobed hepatica, bloodroot, Dutchman's breeches, and marsh marigold are some of the short-lived ephemerals that bloom in the spring at Nerstrand Big Woods. The Minnesota (dwarf) trout lily grows here. In fact, it grows only in Rice and Goodhue counties.

Spring visitors are also treated to the musical return of tufted titmice, blue-gray gnatcatchers, blue-winged warblers, cerulean warblers, and waves of other migrant birds. The repertoires of the kinglet, the robin, and the cardinal accompany the early flora and blend with the sounds of the stream's flowing water.

Prairie Creek is a small descendant of the glacial waters that once excavated this valley, replacing strength with charm. Meandering along the valley bottom, the stream provides habitat for raccoons, deer, foxes, and a host of other animals. The stream gurgles around small boulders and plunges over a limestone ledge.

The hillsides are layered with glacial deposits that obscure the more ancient history of the land. But where the creek encounters bedrock there is more than a moss-covered waterfall: There we can witness ancient geologic history. The bedrock, called the "Platteville Formation," is limestone formed in a warm, shallow sea, far enough away from the shore so that waves couldn't wash over and cover the rock with sand and mud. We know that this area was once teeming with snails, molluscs, trilobites, and large lily-shaped crinoids.

Today the warm ocean currents have been replaced by a changing seasonal spectacle. Spring flowers, mushrooms, and birds are followed by the deep greens and shaded paths of summer. Then a display of rich fall colors yields to a white blanket of snow.

Amidst a landscape of farm fields and small towns, this park is a surprise and a treasure. The trail to Hidden Falls is the most popular walk in the park. However, thirteen more miles of hiking trails provide ample opportunity for solitude and relaxation. People come to picnic, camp, hike, ski, and snowmobile, or just to absorb the beauty of a historic wooded region.

For more information about this park contact: Nerstrand Big Woods State Park, 9700 170th Street E., Nerstrand, MN 55053. Phone 507-334-8848. See also the address for the DNR Information Center at the front of the book.

Fall Color, Sugar Maples (Acer saccharum)
(Greg L. Ryan and Sally A. Beyer)

White Trout Lily (Erythronium albidum) *(Joe Niznik)*

Prairie Creek waterfall, Nerstrand Big Woods State Park (Bob Firth)

SAKATAH LAKE

Sakatah Lake State Park was established in 1963 in response to popular demand. The result was the protection of part of the Big Woods and three and a half miles of Upper Sakatah Lake and Lower Sakatah Lake shoreline.

The hardwoods forest here is a colorful flower garden in the spring and a deep green maze in the summer. Large oaks reach across park roads, forming a leafy arch.

The park has hiking and ski trails, and the Sakatah–Singing Hills Trail traverses through the park. The trail spans forty-two miles of rolling terrain from Mankato to Faribault and is designed to be used by hikers, bicyclists, and snowmobilers. The state trail is on an old railway grade, which provides solid ground and spectacular scenery. In the summer, bicyclists are accompanied by a chorus of ovenbird, pewee, and vireo songs. However, it is autumn, when the trees are ablaze with color, that is for best biking.

Boat access and canoe rentals encourage visitors to explore the lake. Nearby Waterville bills itself as the bullhead capital, and the area attracts many anglers from Iowa, Illinois, and Indiana. There are also walleye, bass, northerns, and panfish in the lake.

Sakatah Lake is a natural beginning for the Cannon River canoe route, which begins on the west side of the lake. The park has an summer interpretive program, camping, picnicking, and a beach for swimmers.

For more information about this park contact: Sakatah Lake State Park, Route 2, Box 19, Waterville, MN 56096. Phone 507–362–4438. See also the address for the DNR Information Center at the front of the book.

Sakatah–Singing Hills State Trail (Minnesota DNR)

THE PRAIRIE PARKS

For Native Americans and early settlers alike, the vast prairies were a significant part of the history of this area. But before the settlers came, lightning-caused and Indian-set fires and uncertain rainfall affected our native grasslands, and without fire the grasslands would have succumbed to overgrowth of brush and trees. Then, the European emigrants came along and sought to farm the land. Plows and progress have been responsible for the demise of the prairies that once covered one-third of the state from the northwest to the southeast corners.

Prairie grasses waved on ancient glacial moraines, till plains, sand plains, wetlands, and southwestern Minnesota's steep slopes. Less than 1 percent of the original Minnesota prairie now exists, found as scattered fragments in state parks, Scientific and Natural Areas, Nature Conservancy preserves, and wildlife management areas. Bison, elk, long-billed curlew, and McCown's longspur are gone; the prairie chicken, Karner blue butterfly, and ball cactus are threatened. Approximately 15 percent of all the state's endangered plants are found in the prairie. Sprague's pipit and Baird's sparrow may not exist in the state any longer.

The higher elevations of prairie are in southwest Minnesota's Coteau des Prairies (highland of the prairie) region, and the low prairies are in the glacial Lake Agassiz bed of northwest Minnesota. Prairie cordgrass and blue jointgrass grow in wetlands, big bluestem and Indian grass often grow in fertile upland soil, and little bluestem and side-oats grama are found on thin, dry soils.

The six state parks included in this section of the book have important prairie species. Many other parks, including O. L. Kipp (its preserve is the best goat prairie in the state), Whitewater, Lindbergh, Upper Sioux Agency, Minneopa, Sakatah Lake, Lake Maria, Beaver Creek Valley, Sibley, Camden, Lake Bronson, Lake Carlos, Maplewood, Fort Snelling, Crow Wing, Fort Ridgely, St. Croix, Wild River, Afton, and Frontenac state parks have prairie management too, although they are included in a different section of the book.

The prairie environment provides two indelible images—a sea of grass waving in the breeze and the floral patterns of late summer.

BLUE MOUNDS

The prairie horizon is broken by a mound, a bluish hump in the distance. Before houses, development, and windbreaks, the landscape was tall grass waving in the wind and a quartzite mound rising from the plains. The explorer-naturalist Joseph Nicollet called this "The Rock." As you get closer, the mound turns red, the color of the ancient sediments that make up the metamorphic bedrock. Prairie grass, then rock terraces, followed by steep cliffs, form the mile-long eastern escarpment. The visitor center is located on the south end of the mound, and is the former home of the novelist Frederick Manfred, writer of historical fiction.

The Dakota Indians came here to hunt bison. Legends say that the bison were driven over the cliff and tell of piles of bones beneath the cliff, but archaeologists have found more interesting artifacts in the area—spearheads and tools, which provide insights into the nomadic lives of the ancient hunters. The bison, which disappeared from the wild in Minnesota over one hundred years ago, are back again. A herd is maintained in large pastures in the park where they graze on prairie grass.

The prairie was nearly eliminated as settlers began moving into the area around 1869. Fires once moved regularly across the landscape, eliminating woody plants and releasing rich nutrients back into the soil. The settlers fought droughts, blizzards, tornadoes, and even locust plagues, but it was fire they feared most. By 1890, the plow had turned enough soil to eliminate the big fires and to change the environment.

On top of the mound the thin soil and hard rock prevented plowing and forestry. As a result, the area has been well preserved as one of our best examples of a natural prairie. While other prairie plots emphasize floral displays, botanists look to Blue Mounds for short and tall grass. Many people also come here to see cacti bloom in June and July. Two species of prickly pear cactus grow here: Western prickly pear has large flat pads and brittle prickly pear has small round pads.

Other special plants are in this park as well. On top of the mound the depression pools (natural indentations in the rock) support four species of rare plants. The ancient sea floor ripple marks provide a growing surface that is very different from the soft glacial soil. Here, blue-green lichens may contribute to the mound's name.

Once part of the prairie wildlife, the coyote was eliminated from the area, but unlike other species it came back to wander along the park's rocky ridge lines. Now campers can listen for the barks and howls of the individual coyote announcing its location to the social group, and the group's howl, a response to the individual.

Blue Mounds State Park is famous among birdwatchers because 225 species are found here. Migrant waterfowl land in the impoundments, Swainson's hawks hunt the prairie, and upland sandpipers and blue grosbeaks are among the specialties found at Blue Mounds.

Besides ideal settings for botanists, birders, anthropologists, ecologists, and historians, there are trails to hike or snowmobile. The visitor center provides learning opportunities. There are modern campgrounds for small or large groups, and areas for picnickers and a beach for swimmers.

For more information about this park contact: Blue Mounds State Park, Route 1, Luverne, MN 56156. Phone 507–283–4892. See also the address for the DNR Information Center at the front of the book.

Bison (Bison bison) *(Dominique Braud)*

Sioux quartzite outcropping, Blue Mounds State Park (Bob Firth)

*Prickly Pear Cactus (*Opuntia macrorhiza*)
(Greg L. Ryan and Sally A. Beyer)*

BUFFALO RIVER

Imagine a blue expanse larger than all the Great Lakes combined, then replace the water with waves of grass, a living sea of summer flowers and green grass. Add nomadic hunters and herds of bison, and put in a string of ox carts carrying goods north and south and east and west. Then, finally, picture the sod being broken and replaced with cropland, and the shooting of the elk and the bison. This is the history of Buffalo River State Park.

Today, people come here to swim in the cool waters of the impoundment on the Buffalo River or to wet a line fishing below the dam. They come to picnic and to camp, but the real significance of the park is its trails. Buffalo River State Park and the adjoining Nature Conservancy Bluestem Prairie Scientific and Natural Area form the largest and best of the state's prairie preserves.

Glacial Lake Agassiz once covered over two hundred thousand square miles; seventeen thousand square miles were in Minnesota. Its waters covered a broad flat plain; when the lake drained it left behind an even flatter basin. One of the lake's beach lines runs through the park. The beach, called Campbell Beach by geologists, represents a significant ridge that runs for over a hundred miles in Minnesota. The beach would not impress anyone as a highland, but it does put a ripple in the prairie, and in a very short distance the flat grasslands move from rich black soil of the lake bed to coarse gravel of the beach. Over 670 plants, many now rare, grow here.

Wildlife enthusiasts can also enjoy the diversity of the area. Birdwatchers look for the prairie chicken. Both the willow and alder flycatchers are here, and the dickcissel reaches the northern limits of its range in this area.

The marbled godwit is a large bird that needs broad expanses of prairie as territory. The bird feeds along the edge of wetlands, where its eight- to thirteen-centimeter bill can probe the mud for food. In 1879, ornithologist T. S. Roberts described these birds as being so abundant and noisy that they were a nuisance. Their slaughter by market hunters and the destruction of the prairie changed that status. Similarly, the upland sandpiper requires large expanses of grassland and was shot for the marketplace at the same time the prairie was being destroyed.

Less conspicuous wildlife rarities include the prairie vole, a small rodent of the dry prairies. The Dakota skipper is a butterfly that is tawny orange above with some yellow below. The skipper has an affinity for purple coneflowers; it sits with wings slightly folded, unlike most butterflies that we observe.

The Buffalo River provides shade and moisture on a hot prairie summer day. A woodland of elm, ash, cottonwood, and oak grows here, attracting many birds and vacationing humans. White-tailed deer, red fox, white-tailed jackrabbit, prairie toads, and numerous beaver dams and cuttings can be found along the river.

There is a visitor center for interpretation of the park's natural history, historic WPA buildings, group camps, cross-country ski trails, and secluded locations where an artist with a brush or a camera can catch the subtle coloration of the prairie landscape.

For more information about this park contact: Buffalo River State Park, Route 2, Box 118, Glyndon, MN 56547. Phone 218–498–2124. See also the address for the DNR Information Center at the front of the book.

Prairie Chicken (Tympanuchus cupido) *(Daniel J. Cox)*

Sandhill Crane (Grus canadensis) *(Walt Huss)*

Bluestem Prairie, Buffalo River State Park (Minnesota DNR)

GLACIAL LAKES

Looking from the top of the scenic glacial hills in Glacial Lakes State Park, you can see beautiful vistas of the surrounding countryside. Prairie wildflowers blanket these landforms; the combination of the wildflowers and the land makes a wonderful outdoor laboratory for geology and botany enthusiasts.

Horseback riding or hiking along the ridge is inspirational, with the wildflowers and grasses rippling in the wind and the setting sun pushing your shadow across the hillside. Bluebirds sit on branches and sparrows call from hidden perches, while hawks ride the thermals up the slopes. This is considered a gravel prairie, where midgrasses such as side-oats grama and little bluestem predominate. A nature trail helps to explain the natural history to hikers.

The oak woodlands shade both the picnic grounds and part of the campgrounds. Some oaks cloak the top of the moraine, but the conical kames that formed from glacial debris are covered with grasses.

An esker is a gravel ridge marking a riverbed that formed within a glacier. In Glacial Lakes State Park an esker runs across from the contact station and forms the ridge for the road and campground. The esker also dams the flow from the runoff and hillside springs and creates the fifty-six-acre Mountain Lake.

With the entire watershed inside the park, this lake is clear and clean. No motors are allowed here, but canoes and row boats can be rented, and fishing and swimming are both fun and refreshing.

For more information about this park contact: Glacial Lakes State Park, Route 2, Box 126, Starbuck, MN 56381. Phone 612–239–2860. See also the address for the DNR Information Center at the front of the book.

Prairie, Glacial Lakes State Park (Joe Niznik)

The word *savanna* has an exotic ring. The word brings to mind African plains, but it also describes the oak-prairie mix on the rolling hills of Myre–Big Island State Park. The Esker Trail in the park leads to an example of the oak savanna lands and vividly shows the effects of the glaciers, which left a landscape of dry uplands, wet lowlands, and ice-block lake basins.

Prairie grasses wave in the wind, and prairie wildflowers glow in the summer sun. Bur oak acorns provide food for wildlife, the trees give shelter to cavity-nesting animals, and the grasslands are pasture for deer. In addition, there is a wetland complex of sedges and cordgrass for marsh wildlife. These wetlands are reservoirs of water—sponges on the landscape. In times of drought, the wetlands protect the watertable and save the landscape from rapid erosion.

Albert Lea Lake was formed by the depression left from melted ice blocks that had been buried in glacial debris. The lake is now a resting area for migrating white pelicans and other waterfowl; the shoreline shrubs provide shelter and perches for migrant song birds. Raccoons forage on the banks, white-tailed deer come to the lake to drink, opossum hide in the forest, muskrats forage in the cattails. The same diversity that attracted wildlife and Native Americans to the area also attracts tourists, and visitors are treated to a glimpse of the historic landscape of southern Minnesota.

Big Island, which was the original park, is now connected to the mainland by a causeway. The island is the site of a deciduous forest that escaped the prairie-building fires of the mainland. On a hillside overlooking the lake is New York Point, the site of the annual Big Island Rendezvous in October.

Owen Johnson Interpretive Center is an active learning center and home to Johnson's outstanding collection of Native American artifacts. The park also includes campgrounds and a good network of trails.

For more information about this park contact: Myre–Big Island State Park, Route 3, Box 33, Albert Lea, MN 56007. Phone 507–373–5084. See also the address for the DNR Information Center at the front of the book.

Big Island Rendezvous, Myre–Big Island State Park (Greg L. Ryan and Sally A. Beyer)

RICE LAKE

Rice Lake is well known locally as a good place to see wildlife, especially in the twilight and in the early morning. This is the most significant waterfowl lake in the area, and consequently it is a gathering spot for people as well. Large flocks of migrating waterfowl stop here on their way to their nesting grounds in the spring and their wintering grounds in the fall.

The lake formed in a depression left by the glacial drift of the ancient Wisconsin Ice Age, a period that dates back over four hundred thousand years. Rice Lake is a shallow lake and forms the headwaters for the middle branch of the Zumbro River. Nesting along the water's edge are redwing blackbirds, the vocal marsh and sedge wrens, and the very shy Virginia rails with their comical call, "kidick-kidick-wuffle-wuffle-wuffle." The woodland of the peninsula is home to a variety of woodpeckers.

People have had a long history here. The Native Americans harvested wild rice from the lake. Later, the mill owners on the Zumbro River, east of the present park area, constructed dikes and dams to channel the water their way. Today, people enjoy the woodlands as a place for hiking, picnicking, and viewing wildflowers. Visitors come here to relax, swim, visit, and to explore a wildlife oasis in the midst of farmland.

For more information about this park contact: Rice Lake State Park, Route 3, Box 45, Owatonna, MN 55060. Phone 507–451–7406. See also the address for the DNR Information Center at the front of the book.

Great Egret (Casmerodius albus) (Walt Huss)

Split Rock Creek State Park is in a region of Minnesota known as the Coteau des Prairies. The park derives its name from a creek that flows through quartzite dells along its route. This small park is important to Pipestone County because it has the only lake and one of the largest woodlots in the county.

Quartzite is exposed by a dam, built in 1938, on the park's south side, and the stream forms a lake behind the dam. A campground and a picnic area are located next to the lake; both are shaded by ash trees, which were planted shortly after the dam was constructed. A hillside of remnant prairie slopes toward the lake, and a visitor center helps people understand and appreciate the grassland.

Park users can cool off at the beach, or launch a boat to fish for perch, crappie, sunfish, or walleye. The picnic area receives lots of family use. In both spring and fall, the lake is a good place to observe waterfowl—April is the best month to see ducks in their breeding plumage. Birdwatchers should check the woodlands too. The lack of trees on most of the Coteau des Prairies makes this a popular stop for songbirds passing through. During the summer, western kingbirds and orchard orioles are special residents. The winter months offer ice skating, ice fishing, and cross-country skiing.

For more information about this park contact: Split Rock Creek State Park, Route 2, Jasper, MN 56144. Phone 507–348–7908. See also the address for the DNR Information Center at the front of the book.

Split Rock Lake, Split Rock Creek State Park (Bill Rooks)

THE LAKE PARKS

Minnesota's most famous resource is its water. Over fifteen thousand lakes cover 8 percent of the state, and 90 percent of all Minnesotans live within two miles of a lake. Including rivers, water in Minnesota covers three million acres. The lakes range from Lake Superior's 1,330-foot depth to the shallow potholes of the prairie. They support over 150 species of fish, plus waterfowl and furbearers.

Lakes of the Rainy River and Lake Superior regions are found in the glacially scoured Precambrian Shield, or in the glacial deposits of the Rainy Lobe, and tend to be cold, deep, and clear. Most are connected to swift-flowing streams, and rainfall usually exceeds evaporation, so the streams are active all year. Bear Head Lake, McCarthy Beach, Tettegouche, and Scenic state parks all preserve northern lakes.

The greatest concentration of lakes in Minnesota is on moraines such as the Alexandria in the west central part of Minnesota, with Lake Carlos, Monson, Maplewood, Glacial Lakes, and Sibley state parks; the smaller Nickerson Moraine near Duluth includes Moose Lake State Park; the St. Croix Moraine in the east central part of the state supports Lake Maria State Park.

Some state parks have reservoir lakes such as Hayes Lake and Lake Bronson. In addition to the North Shore parks, Zippel Bay on Lake of the Woods, Father Hennepin on Mille Lacs, McCarthy Beach, Lake Bemidji, Myre–Big Island, and Lake Shetek state parks are among those that protect a portion of the shorelines on large lakes. In Maplewood and Bear Head Lake state parks, numerous lakes are protected.

A few aquatic species are on Minnesota's endangered flora and fauna list, but for the most part our lakes are still in good condition and deserve our continual monitoring and protection.

The Lake Parks

Bear Head Lake

Father Hennepin

Hayes Lake

Lake Bronson

Lake Carlos

Lake Shetek

Maplewood *(Hidden Gem)*

McCarthy Beach

Monson Lake

Moose Lake

Scenic

Sibley *(Major Park)*

Zippel Bay *(Hidden Gem)*

Bear Head Lake is a spectacular 674-acre lake completely within the park boundaries. The woods are made up of red and white pine, spruce, fir, and paper birch on the highlands; tamarack, black spruce, and white cedar comprise the lowland vegetation. Small, clear trout lakes are set in a rugged terrain or volcanic bedrock and glacial sediment. Among the animals found in the park are moose, black bears, timber wolves, bald eagles, red-breasted nuthatches, pine grosbeaks, red crossbills, and boreal chickadees. What does this description suggest? Canoe country!

Bear Head Lake State Park is in the boreal forest. The park provides a sample of the wild beauty that attracts over one hundred thousand visitors to the Boundary Waters Canoe Area Wilderness each year. The DNR stocks the park's trout lakes; Bear Head Lake also has walleye to tempt the angler.

Fortunately, road access is confined to the middle of the park, but exploration is not. There are miles of cross-country skiing and hiking trails. In addition, the Taconite State Trail, which cuts across the park, provides access for snowmobilers, horseback riders, and hikers.

Daytime visitors can picnic, swim at a sandy beach, walk on short trails, rent a canoe, or fish. For longer stays there are even more options. Small backcountry lakes have backpack campsites, and there are two boat access campsites on Bear Head Lake. The other campgrounds vary from modern to rustic, and there is a separate group camp.

For more information about this park contact: Bear Head Lake State Park, Star Route 2, Box 5700, Ely, MN 55731. Phones 218–365–4253 and 218–365–3150. See also the address for the DNR Information Center at the front of the book.

Cub Lake, Bear Head Lake State Park (Greg L. Ryan and Sally A. Beyer)

FATHER HENNEPIN

Father Hennepin State Park is located on Mille Lacs Lake. Mille Lacs is the second largest lake that is completely within the border of Minnesota, but it is less than fifty feet deep. Two little rocky islands northwest of the park form a natural wildlife refuge for nesting birds, and the surrounding waters support nesting walleye. The park is a "headlands," a natural highland, on the west side of Isle Bay.

There are short cross-country ski, snowmobile, and hiking trails in the park, but the emphasis is on the lake, with a popular beach and two boat launches. The wooded picnic areas, the large campgrounds, and the playgrounds provide park users with recreational options to accompany overnight camping, a day at the beach, or a serious fishing experience.

Northerns, bluegills, crappie, bass, walleye, and muskies are all found in the lake. Osprey, loons, eagles, terns, cormorants, and mergansers look for smaller rough fish, while anglers search for large game fish. The urge to fish does not subside with summer. Fall brings muskie and northern enthusiasts, and in the winter the thousands of ice houses resemble a city on the tundra.

For more information about this park contact: Father Hennepin State Park, Box 397, Isle, MN 56342. Phone 612–676–8763. See also the address for the DNR Information Center at the front of the book.

Father Hennepin State Park
(Dan Wennberg/Firth Photobank)

Hayes Lake State Park is adjacent to Beltrami Island State Forest and offers a quiet backcountry wilderness atmosphere. Located in the glacial Lake Agassiz plains, the park offers pine woodlands at the edge of the prairie and farmland, plus a lake for swimming and fishing.

The North Fork of the Roseau River flows through the park, and its waters fill Hayes Lake, a meandering reservoir. Water for the Roseau River filters through the bogs of the old lake bed where they are colored by tannin. This large filter gives the river and the lake high quality water. Crappie, sunfish, and northerns prosper here. There is also a population of bass in the lake.

Under the jack pines, visitors collect blueberries by the bucketful. They can also see a tremendous assortment of orchids in the early summer and gentians in late summer. Birdwatchers find a bonanza here with nearly two hundred species in or around the park. Western prairie species, including the black-billed magpie, have nests in the area; northern conifer forest birds, like the crossbill, live here too. Because the park borders some of the wildest lands in Minnesota, visitors may also encounter wolves, bears, or moose.

The park receives daytime use from surrounding communities and the campgrounds are often crowded. Hiking, cross-country skiing, snowmobiling, and equestrian trails connect with the surrounding state forest. The lake is the park's magnet. Canoes and boats with electric motors can use Hayes Lake, although beaver dams and downed trees make the remainder of the river difficult to travel on.

For more information about this park contact: Hayes Lake State Park, Star Route 4, Box 84, Roseau, MN 56751. Phone 218–425–7504. See also the address for the DNR Information Center at the front of the book.

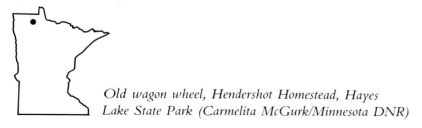

Old wagon wheel, Hendershot Homestead, Hayes Lake State Park (Carmelita McGurk/Minnesota DNR)

LAKE BRONSON

The South Branch of the Two Rivers fills Lake Bronson, which provides fishing, swimming, and an ideal backdrop for the picnic grounds in Lake Bronson State Park. The lake, actually a reservoir, was developed after the 1930s drought dried up the wells in the local communities. A dam, built by the WPA, was placed where the river cut through the McCauleyville Beach line, and now it is the region's greatest attraction. The WPA also built several other magnificent structures in the park.

Fishing for walleye, northerns, perch, or bass; hiking the woods; or sitting in the picnic grounds and enjoying the breeze are all favorites of park users. The picnic tables sit within a forest of young oak trees, where birds like to perch in the branches.

On the ground patches of deep green mingle with the light-colored grasses. The deep green plant is a shrub called creeping juniper and is found on rocky outcrops, beach dunes, and old beach lines. Creeping juniper is a pioneer plant that flourished on the glacial Lake Agassiz beaches and struggles to exist today.

The park is on the margin of the deciduous forest and the prairie. It has a sizable bird, mammal, reptile, and amphibian population with deer and sharp-tailed grouse among the most abundant. Surprisingly, this may be the best park in the state to see moose, eagles, and sandhill cranes.

There are 190 individual campsites and a group campground. A snack bar, boat and canoe rental, and interpretive program are available seasonally. There are hiking, snowmobile, cross-country ski, and bicycle trails. A historic observation tower rises above the trees. Anglers enjoy spear fishing in the winter.

For more information about this park contact: Lake Bronson State Park, Box 9, Lake Bronson, MN 56734. Phone 218–754–2200. See also the address for the DNR Information Center at the front of the book.

Historic Civilian Conservation Corps (CCC) observation tower, Lake Bronson State Park (Carmelita McGurk/Minnesota DNR)

Lake Carlos State Park protects a valuable natural area of woods, prairie, and potholes, but it is the one and a half miles of Lake Carlos shoreline that attracts the visitors. Over three hundred lakes are in the Alexandria area, and in the park there is a ramp which makes beautiful Lake Carlos accessible.

The glacial material in the lake and gravel pit is made up of rounded rock that has been sorted into distinct layers. This would indicate a moving water deposit and the gradual filling of a valley by glacial runoff. Today's surface waters run into the Long Prairie River.

A variety of recreational activities revolve around the lake. Lake Carlos is 163 feet deep with fourteen miles of shoreline and many shallow areas for northerns and drop-offs for walleye. Many anglers participate in a catch-and-release program to maintain high quality fishing. Visitors use the lake for water-skiing, cruising, as well as angling. The park has a beach at the picnic grounds and a lakeshore campgrounds.

Smaller lakes and ponds are included in the park. An interpretive trail tells about the wetlands, and Hidden Lake provides a scenic setting for the group camp. Beautiful forest trails lead hikers through a rich woodland. Outstanding horseback, hiking, skiing, and snowmobile trails lead to secluded areas of the park.

Lake Carlos, Lake Carlos State Park (Joe Niznik)

For more information about this park contact: Lake Carlos State Park, Route 2, Box 240, Carlos, MN 56319. Phone 612–852–7200. See also the address for the DNR Information Center at the front of the book.

LAKE SHETEK

Explorer Joseph Nicollet camped for three days by Lake Shetek in 1838. In his journal he noted that the Dakota called the lake "Rabechy," which meant it was the nesting place for pelicans. The name "Shetek" is from the Ojibwe and also means "pelican." In a land of grasslands and farm fields where shallow ponds are the rule and large lakes almost nonexistent, Lake Shetek is a significant landmark.

Lake Shetek, the source of the Des Moines River, is also the source of much pride and pleasure for the local residents and an attraction for tourists. With the aid of aeration each winter preventing winterkill, the lake has become a place for excellent fishing.

Pelicans still stop here, yellow-billed cuckoos and willow flycatchers can be found in the woods, and migrant waterfowl use all the lakes. Beaver, muskrat, squirrel, and deer inhabit the area. Loon Island is a forty-five-acre nature preserve that can be reached by crossing a causeway built in the late 1930s by WPA workers.

Although much of the park itself is wooded, Shetek and connecting lakes make up nearly four thousand acres of water. Walleye, northern, crappie, and bullhead fishing is good. Other park features include two stocked fishing ponds, a swimming beach, picnic grounds, boat and canoe rental, and a group center. A log cabin dates to the mid 1800s, and a monument commemorates fifteen people from six families that died in the U.S.–Dakota Conflict of 1862. Today, campers, and family reunions populate the park. A full-time summer naturalist program and a variety of hiking, skiing, and snowmobile trails enhance the public's enjoyment of the park.

Historic Andrew Koch Cabin, Lake Shetek State Park (Bill Rooks)

For more information about this park contact: Lake Shetek State Park, Route 1, Box 164, Currie, MN 56123. Phone 507–763–3256. See also the address for the DNR Information Center at the front of the book.

MAPLEWOOD

In Maplewood State Park hills, lakes, woodlands, marshes, and prairies give park users a wide variety of activities to choose from: swimming, horseback riding, camping, and picnicking. Maplewood is nine thousand acres of beautiful rolling hills, but ranks in the second half of the park list for attendance. Often there are more Dakota license plates than Minnesota plates.

On the edge of the Red River valley, the Alexandria Moraine rises into higher and more dramatic relief, and is home to over forty lakes. The lakes and ponds fill many depressions (or kettles). The conical hills are called kames and, like the kettles, were formed by the melting of the glaciers. Maplewood State Park, located on the moraine, is a textbook example of kettle and kame topography. Glacial Lakes State Park is also an excellent example of this topography.

The lakes provide good fishing and boating, and boat landings and canoe campsites are in the park. Despite its name, Bass Lake is the park's trout lake. Its waters are cold, clean, and well oxygenated, so rainbow trout do well here.

Not all the lakes in this area are deep. Grassy Lake got its name because it dried up in the 1930s during a drought, and hay was harvested in its basin. This lake is still affected by drought and is susceptible to winterkill when the snow builds up on the ice and prevents sunlight penetration. Shallow depressions left by the glaciers created swamps and marshes instead of lakes. Beavers impound water in some of the swamps and marshes, creating good sites for wildlife observation.

The kames are home to a variety of natural communities, complementing the wetlands. As a result of the varied landscape, 150 bird species breed in the park, along with fifty species of mammals, and twenty-five kinds of reptiles and amphibians. The park staff has identified thirteen plant communities within the park's borders. The park includes several deer exclosures that let observers know how much impact browsing deer have on the forest.

The woodland trails offer spring floral displays, and the grasslands flower in summer. Visitors can enjoy trillium and two kinds of hepatica, wild onion, and prairie rose. The fall colors along the scenic park drive are spectacular.

Monarch butterflies float above patches of milkweed, dragonflies cruise the swamps, kingbirds hunt from open perches, and swallows feed in large flocks. Cuckoos, cerulean warblers, and blue-gray gnatcatchers can be found in the park.

There is a variety of camping sites, overlooks, and trails to choose from. The park drive is best for wildlife observation at dawn and dusk, especially observation of deer. In the winter, fourteen miles of ski trails, seventeen miles of snowmobile trails, and ice fishing are available. If adventure calls, snowshoers and skiers can winter camp using the trail Adirondack shelters.

For more information about this park contact: Maplewood State Park, Route 3, Box 422, Pelican Rapids, MN 56572. Phone 218-863-8383. See also the address for the DNR Information Center at the front of the book.

Maplewood State Park (Joe Niznik)

42

Maplewood State Park (Joe Gartner/Minnesota DNR)

Raccoon (Procyon lotor) *(Minnesota DNR)*

McCARTHY BEACH

The majority of visitors to this park never see the largest part of McCarthy Beach State Park. It's hard to leave the beauty and comfort of the sandy beach and conifer-studded picnic grounds on Sturgeon Lake and the wooded campground on Side Lake.

The park adjoins a chain of lakes that can be traveled by boat. The narrow strip of land that separates Sturgeon and Side lakes is the most developed part of the park. A boat ramp and information office complete the facilities.

Beyond this strip, the road crosses a mix of private land and state park. The landscape is rolling and sandy, with large stands of red and white pine. There are also small lakes and leatherleaf–black spruce lowlands in the less-developed portions of the park.

This part of the country had many large stands of pines when the first sawmill started up. Today such a pineland is quite unusual and significant. The people who enjoy the backcountry are snowmobilers who use the three miles of the Taconite State Trail that dissect the forest, cross-country skiers who enjoy crisscrossing the mixed terrain, and hikers who enjoy the loons, warblers, and orchids.

The park is located at the midpoint of the Taconite State Trail. It is seventy miles to Grand Rapids and ninety-five miles to Ely on the state trail, but it is much closer to the open pits and taconite country at Chisholm and Ironworld.

This park mixes well with its surroundings. The park represents development where there are campgrounds and resorts, and it represents wilderness where it blends with the George Washington and Sturgeon River state forests.

For more information about this park contact: McCarthy Beach State Park, HCR 5, Box 341, Hibbing, MN 55746. Phone 218–254–2411. See also the address for the DNR Information Center at the front of the book.

McCarthy Beach State Park (Connie Wanner)

MONSON LAKE

Slip a canoe into Monson Lake. Cast a lure for northerns, bass, walleye, or panfish. Glide along the shore and listen to house wrens and blackbirds sing. Explore a short portage that leads from Monson Lake to West Sunburg Lake. Fishing is a popular autumn activity at Monson Lake, and a quiet campground and a wooded picnic grounds complete the amenities of the memorial park.

Monson Lake State Park was established as a memorial to the members of the Broberg and Lundberg families that perished here. The families were among the first victims of the only U.S.–Dakota Indian war in Minnesota. The solitude of the park is a fitting tribute to the pioneers and the Dakota who were all caught in a confusing policy of treaty and expansion.

In the right season at East Monson Lake (outside the park), you can watch the mating dance of western grebes as they arch their bodies out of the water and run along the surface. White pelicans and herons are found here too.

For more information about this park contact: Monson Lake State Park, Sunburg, MN 56289. Phone 612–366–3797. See also the address for the DNR Information Center at the front of the book.

Monson Lake State Park (Connie Wanner)

MOOSE LAKE

Moose Lake State Park (Connie Wanner)

Moose Lake State Park is a comfortable, pastoral park. It is the kind of place that we think about for a variety of activities: taking the folks on a picnic, letting the kids romp in the lake or play volleyball while the adults pitch horseshoes, casting a line in the water, and sitting and "shooting the breeze."

The area around Moose Lake State Park is a glacial landscape of outwash (flowing meltwater) and buried ice blocks (kettle lakes). This park is a mix of fields and woods, woodland wildlife ponds, and fishing lakes. It is shade and sunlight, breezes off Echo Lake, and grassy campsites. There are walleye, northerns, and panfish in Echo and Moosehead lakes, and picnic tables near the beach by Echo Lake.

The rolling hills are gently sloped for easy strolls and casual skiing. In the evening white-tailed deer browse in the grassy fields, geese and ducks rise and settle again on the ponds, and bird songs vary from field to swale.

Snowmobile trails connect with two county-wide networks. The park borders the community of Moose Lake and Interstate 35.

For more information about this park contact: Moose Lake State Park, Route 2, 1000 County 137, Moose Lake, MN 55767. Phones 218–485–4059 and 218–384–4610. See also the address for the DNR Information Center at the front of the book.

Scenic State Park was established in 1921 in response to local demand to preserve the beautiful virgin pines along the six lakeshores within the park. The clear northern lakes provide fishing, boating, swimming, relief from summer heat, and glimpses of wildlife. Loons, eagles, osprey, mergansers, and goldeneyes are seen regularly. Otters, moose, and beavers are more difficult to spot. Birders consider this one of the best places in the state to see the hard-to-find spruce grouse.

The habitats are varied because of the many land forms left by the Rainy and Grantsburg–Des Moines lobes of the last glaciation. An esker forms the winding and steep-sided peninsula called Chase Point. Two bends in the glacial river are preserved by this sandy ridge. Morainic deposits and kames give the landscape its rolling relief. The lakes were formed by depressions, tunnel valleys, and buried ice blocks.

Coon and Sandwick lakes are the most popular places in the park. There are trails around them, boat-in campsites, and a beach. Fishing is great for walleye, northerns, bass, and panfish. Motorboat speeds on the lakes are limited to under ten miles per hour.

Park accommodations range from a rental lakeshore cabin, to campsites with electrical hookups, to backcountry backpack sites. Five miles of trail is devoted to interpretation. In addition, there are hiking, cross-country ski, and snowmobile trails. A historic lodge with displays and naturalist programs, boat rentals, and a forest fire tower add variety. The park is surrounded by state and national forests, and the Bigfork River is nearby.

For more information about this park contact: Scenic State Park, Route 2, Bigfork, MN 56628. Phone 218–743–3362. See also the address for the DNR Information Center at the front of the book.

Bald Eagle (Haliaeetus leucocephalus) *(Walt Huss)*

SIBLEY

The view from Mount Tom is not what it used to be. In fact, the view from Mount Tom has been constantly changing since prairie grasses flowed down its flanks and all the way to the Rocky Mountains.

Mount Tom is the highest point in a fifty-mile radius and the tallest spot on the Alexandria Moraine complex. Broken pieces of stone pipes have led archaeologists to speculate that the Dakota Indians might have come here on vision quests.

The silent sentinel, Mount Tom, saw the prairies turn to pasture and cropland, the Dakotas disappear, and the towns grow. Villagers hiked Mount Tom's slopes and had picnics long before the area became park.

Eventually, prairie fires were eliminated and so were the deer and elk. From 1880 to 1931, no deer were found here, except for three in a private game park. Change continued as wolves disappeared from the region and woodlands took over.

Times change, and in 1919, Lake Andrew and Mount Tom became part of a designated state park, and the park's role as a natural resource altered the area. A Veteran's Conservation Corps group put up buildings that still are used today. In the 1930s the deer returned to the park. In an old issue of the New London Times a headline read, "Herman Streed SEEN two DEER." Now the park has an abundant population of deer, beavers, foxes, skunks, badgers, muskrats, and squirrels. Waterfowl use the ponds, prairies are being restored, and bird life is diverse. Loons breed and nest on the small lakes within Sibley.

Today, Mount Tom gets thousands of tourists. School children and visitors also stop at the visitor center to learn more about the environment. The year-round naturalist program gives Sibley State Park a special significance as a voice of education, as well as a preserve and playground.

There are family campgrounds, modern group centers, horseback camps, picnic areas, and a swimming beach. Lake Andrew gets the most use, but there are over thirty lakes and ponds within or bordering the park, and portages connect three of the lakes for canoers and anglers. Boat rentals help visitors explore the lake. The kinds of trails to choose among include paved bikeway, hiking, horseback, skiing, and snowmobile. Other features include a spring children's festival, a fall folk art festival, a sliding hill, and a road and trail to the summit of Mount Tom. In the winter, Sibley provides educational and recreational opportunities in a beautiful snow-covered setting.

For more information about this park contact: Sibley State Park, 800 Sibley Park Road NE, New London, MN 56273. Phone 612–354–2055. See also the address for the DNR Information Center at the front of the book.

Marsh Marigold
(Caltha palustris) (Joe Niznik)

49

*Interpretive Trail Center, Sibley State Park
(Dick Clayton/Minnesota DNR)*

Sibley State Park (Dick Clayton/Minnesota DNR)

Zippel Bay is on the southern end of Lake of the Woods. It is eighty miles to the northern shore of the lake in Canada, and hundreds of islands dot the lake. The three-mile-long beach at Zippel Bay is tan, with pieces of white limestone and an assortment of glacial pebbles, which have been washed and rolled by the waves of Lake of the Woods. On some days the surf roars in on northerly winds. The waves pick up strength along the fifteen-mile stretch of open water on the south end of the lake, and the waves foam and race across the shoreline. On other days, there is a glassy tranquility on Lake of the Woods, with boats and distant islands distorted by heat waves or fog. The "mood" of this big lake changes dramatically with the weather, rarely staying the same.

Zippel Bay is the only state park on Lake of the Woods. A remnant of the glacial Lake Agassiz, the present lake has sixty-five thousand miles of shoreline and fourteen thousand islands. Both the U.S. and Canada share ownership of the lake's waters. Zippel Bay was named for a fisherman who settled near the park in 1887. By 1909 he was living in a small hamlet and using the protective bay for harbor, just as today's park users do.

Birds use these protected areas too. Sandhill cranes nest in the bay's marshlands, and the endangered piping plover attempts to breed and raise young on sandy stretches. A Scientific and Natural Area Sanctuary on Curry and Pine islands has been set up for the piping plover, but the bird is still severely threatened with ex-

tinction. People must keep a good distance from the birds during breeding season.

Shorebirds, gulls, terns, eagles, ospreys, and cormorants are part of the lake's treasure. Inland, the forests comprise thick birch stands with white trunks that light up the forest understory. Tanagers, vireos, nuthatches, chickadees, and thrushes live in the forested areas. Moose, wolves, marten, and fishers are part of a diverse but sometimes elusive mammal population. Deer, chipmunks, and squirrels are the most common mammals.

Blueberry patches are everywhere, especially on rocky outcrops and dry ridges, attracting both bears and humans. These ridges break up the flat Agassiz landscape and add interest to the park. Some ridges are exposed bedrock. Precambrian rocks, part of the Canadian Shield, can be found here. The rocks are granitelike and the patterns on them capture the dramatic melting and metamorphosing that have taken place in the last billion and a half years. Other ridges are old beach lines that were established when the lake was higher.

A number of Native American tribes have lived along these shores throughout history. When Pierre de La Verendrye opened Lake of the Woods to the fur trade and established Fort St. Charles, he recorded four tribes living nearby.

Traders came for pelts, and Lake of the Woods was part of a watery highway that connected Lake Superior and Lake Athabasca. Later, more commercial fishermen came, and today sport an-

glers frequent the lake.

The lake is famous for walleye and sauger. There are northerns in the weedy bays, smallmouth bass, perch, muskies, and sturgeon. The sturgeon get less attention than the other fish, but at the end of Zippel Bay, there was a caviar and sturgeon steak fishery around 1900. Today the park offers trails for hiking and horseback riding, boating, camping, swimming, and picnicking.

For more information about this park contact: Zippel Bay State Park, Williams, MN 56686. Phone 218–783–6252. See also the address for the DNR Information Center at the front of the book.

Gull tracks (Bryce Anderson/Minnesota DNR)

Lake of the Woods, Zippel Bay State Park (Greg L. Ryan and Sally A. Beyer)

Ring-billed Gull (Larus delawarensis) (Stephen Maxson/Minnesota DNR)

THE NORTH SHORE OF LAKE SUPERIOR PARKS

The Lake Superior coastline in northern Minnesota is a landscape of rugged volcanic rock and splashing water. Rushing through narrow gorges and plunging over dramatic waterfalls, water drains from the wetlands of the border lakes into Lake Superior. There, water from the surrounding headlands meets the water in the world's largest freshwater lake. The climate of this region is modified by the temperature of the big lake and the south-facing slopes that catch the sun's rays.

Because of the loggers, only a few large pine stands are now left, and the forest is mainly aspen and birch with wetland conifers and deer-pruned white cedar. Logging has changed the landscape and introduced deer to the shoreline. Large deer yards can be found at Gooseberry Falls, Split Rock Lighthouse, and Cascade River state parks.

The newest state park, Grand Portage, includes the spectacular Pigeon River cataracts that made a long portage around the river necessary for past and present explorers. On the southernmost end of the North Shore, the St. Louis River forms the quiet harbor of Duluth after a turbulent trip through Jay Cooke State Park. These rapids forced the voyageurs to establish the first "Grand Portage" (in what is now Jay Cooke State Park) to navigate around the St. Louis River.

Grand Portage National Monument, the Lake Superior Hiking Trail, the North Shore ski trails, and the North Shore snowmobile trail are all part of the North Shore experience, and are interconnected with many state park units.

The North Shore of Lake Superior Parks
Cascade River
Gooseberry Falls *(Major Park)*
Grand Portage
Jay Cooke
Judge C. R. Magney
Split Rock Lighthouse *(Major Park)*
Temperance River
Tettegouche

The Cascade River is aptly named. In the last three miles of its journey to Lake Superior, the river leaps down one ledge after another for a total drop of nine hundred feet. A narrow, black volcanic canyon confines the river and whips the water into bubbling white foam and fine droplets of spray.

Visitors standing on the footbridge that spans the river, or at one of the viewing spots above the river, feel the vibrations of the rushing torrent. This is a boreal rain forest setting, with lush moss and ferns growing on the dripping rock walls. Crystal beads of water hang from the tips of fir needles.

Cascade River State Park covers 2,813 acres, and visitors have ample access to the park's variety and hidden treasure. There are eighteen miles of hiking trails, seventeen miles of cross-country ski trails, two miles of snowmobile trails, and six and a half miles of Lake Superior shoreline. For the ambitious hiker, two trails lead to the forested tops of Moose Mountain and Lookout Mountain.

Wildlife abounds in this hilly terrain. Hikers are serenaded by the sweet chorus of warblers and chickadees. Cross-country skiers may see the tracks of a wolf pack or of deer. This is part of northern Minnesota's largest winter deer yard. Deer browse, seek shelter on the south-facing slopes, and find relief from the deep snow of the interior.

Trailheads provide access to the Superior Hiking Trail and the North Shore State Trail. After a day on the trail, campers can relax in the semi-modern campground or picnic areas. Anglers enjoy shore casting into Lake Superior at the mouth of the Cascade River, as well as stream trout fishing. River activities, hiking, skiing, and camping are popular recreational opportunities offered to North Shore explorers.

For more information about this park contact: Cascade River State Park, HCR 3, Box 450, Lutsen, MN 55612. Phones 218–387–1543 and 218–226–3539. See also the address for the DNR Information Center at the front of the book.

Cascade River, Cascade River State Park (Ronald Morreim)

GOOSEBERRY FALLS

The Gooseberry River plunges over a series of waterfalls, each waterfall marking a different lava flow. During the Precambrian Period, a large rift, or crack, opened in the Lake Superior basin and allowed lava to escape to the surface in massive flows. The flows were not continuous; each flow became a layer of rock by cooling separately and developing its own structure and form. The waterfalls are what visitors come to see at Gooseberry Falls.

For many motorists, Gooseberry Falls State Park is a wayside rest with spectacular scenery. A bridge crosses the deep gorge, and the Upper Falls seem to be right outside the car window. From the bridge, visitors can see patterns in the rock below, the tops of tightly packed columns. The space between each column is a weak spot where water can seep in. When the water freezes, it expands, wedging the outermost column away.

Along Lake Superior, visitors are exposed to a combination of volcanic headlands and cobblestone beaches. Waves explode against the seemingly indestructible bedrock and tumble the cobblestones as if they were piles of marbles. The shoreline is a colorful rock garden, with orange and green lichens coating the slabs of rock, while ninebark, three-leaved cinquefoil, and harebell grow in the cracks. Herring gulls nest on these rocks, while loons and mergansers swim off shore.

Gooseberry Falls State Park has modern campsites and a group camp, three picnic areas, five waterfalls, and five trails. Hikers and skiers can also access the Superior Hiking Trail and the North Shore State Trail at Gooseberry Falls. Most winter visitors come to cross-country ski and snowshoe. The falls are still active in the winter, but are draped with a curtain of ice. The ice sculpture changes throughout the season.

In a winter deer yard in the park, the snow is crisscrossed by the tracks of snowshoe hares, minks, red squirrels, weasels, mice, shrews, and voles.

The Gooseberry River appeared on maps as early as 1670 and may have been named for Sieur des Groseilliers. He and Pierre Esprit Radisson were the first Europeans to explore Lake Superior for the fur trade. Commercial fishing began in the 1870s and logging was established along the river in the 1890s. By 1920, two major fires (in 1909 and 1910) and logging had nearly eliminated the pines. What had been a large white pine forest became a mixed forest of conifer, aspen, and birch. Although the park is now heavily reforested, only stumps remain to remind us of the giant trees that once grew here.

In 1933, the state park was established, and in the 1930s, the CCC built many of the stone structures that are used today. In 1941, the CCC camp closed. Today these stone buildings remain as classic examples of the rustic style of architecture that was used for many Minnesota state park buildings, and blend well with the park's natural environment. Visitor facilities have been updated regularly and today Gooseberry is the most visited park in the state.

For more information about this park contact: Gooseberry Falls State Park, 1300 Highway 61 E., Two Harbors, MN 55616. Phones 218-834-3855 and 218-834-3787. See also the address for the DNR Information Center at the front of the book.

Lake Superior (Bob Firth)

Sunrise, Lake Superior (Paul Sundberg)

Lower Falls, Gooseberry River, Gooseberry River State Park (Greg L. Ryan and Sally A. Beyer)

Minnesota's newest park is on the Canadian border and contains the rapids, waterfalls, cliffs, and rugged terrain that made the nine-mile-long Grand Portage necessary.

The Pigeon River was named for the passenger pigeon by the Ojibwe Indians. The French explorer, Pierre de La Verendrye, included the Pigeon on his 1730 map. Verendrye was the premier explorer of the region and may have been the first non–Native American to use the portage. High Falls, a ninety- to one hundred-foot plunge, is the termination of twenty miles of falls and cascades that begin at the end of the Grand Portage and the site of Fort Charlotte. The wild waters are known as Big Falls (or High Falls or Pigeon Falls), Middle Falls, Horn Rapids, the Cascades, and Partridge Falls.

The park is designed for daytime use rather than camping, with hiking trails and spectacular overlooks. An old log flume on the Canadian side is a historic remnant of the lumber era.

Near the park are Grand Portage National Monument, Verendrye Provincial Park, Middle Falls Provincial Park, and the Grand Portage Reservation. In addition, the park is a reminder of a long and peaceful border between two countries and of the importance of our parks and wild places.

For more information about this park contact: See the address for the DNR Information Center at the front of the book.

High Falls, Pigeon River, Grand Portage State Park
(Paul Wannarka)

JAY COOKE

The St. Louis River led the voyageurs from Lake Superior to the inland lakes and rivers of Minnesota. Present-day Jay Cooke State Park includes the Grand Portage Trail of the St. Louis River. Moccasin-clad feet carried canoe and pack over steep hills of clay on the Grand Portage trail and on trails where today's hiker can travel from the highway into the wilderness.

The river is the showplace of the park, with rapids that are a complex maze of tilted slate and graywacke. The river divides and reunites in powerful canyons and cataracts, while the woods embrace hikers and skiers. The river-carved landscape takes the visitor through the clay beds of glacial Lake Duluth to the very foundations of the ancient Penokean Mountains.

Jay Cooke is linked to Duluth by the Willard Munger Trail, which is very popular with bicyclists. Hiking trails satisfy any type of explorer, and classifications for the trails range from easy to difficult. This is a park with spectacular wildflowers in the spring, colorful stands of northern hardwoods in the fall, and deep snows in the winter.

A person can spend hours on the swinging bridge watching and listening to the current, or move into the backcountry to observe beaver, porcupine, and deer. You can hike or backpack, snowmobile or ski. If backcountry campsites aren't for you, Jay Cooke State Park has a modern campground, two picnic areas, and one of the state's most spectacular overlooks on Highway 23.

Trout fishing, a historic cemetery, beautiful fall colors, the gorge at the Thomson Dam, and the park's geology and natural history present visitors with the challenging task of deciding where and how to spend their time.

For more information about this park contact: Jay Cooke State Park, 500 E. Highway 210, Carlton, MN 55718. Phone 218–384–4610. See also the address for the DNR Information Center at the front of the book.

St. Louis River, Jay Cooke State Park (Bob Firth)

Judge C. R. Magney State Park has more than six miles of trails. The most popular hike leads from the highway back to Devil's Kettle, where the Brule River splits around a mass of volcanic rock. Half of the river plunges fifty feet into a pool, while the rest pours into a huge pothole. Some say that the water in the pothole disappears forever because the outlet is a mystery.

A short distance downstream, tea-colored water shoots over Upper Falls and sets up a curtain of mist. In the winter, a dome of ice builds at the base of this waterfall and muffles the sound of the river.

The Brule River and its tributary, Gauthier Creek, provide anglers with brook and rainbow trout, which are stocked annually by the DNR. Steelhead trout spawn in the river in spring and salmon run in the fall.

While walking along the trail that parallels the river, listen for the songs of warblers in spring and summer. Chickadees, nuthatches, jays, woodpeckers, and ruffed grouse are found in the park all year.

Moose, white-tailed deer, black bears, and timber wolves are the larger animals that inhabit the park. Watch for their tracks or scat on the trails. Smaller mammals—the woodchuck, snowshoe hare, red squirrel, and chipmunk—are seen frequently in the park. Judge C. R. Magney State Park has a rustic campground that is one of the quietest and most relaxing in the state. Spring and fall are good times to find solitude.

Bois Brule State Park was changed to Judge C. R. Magney in 1963 to honor the man who spent much of his life establishing eleven state parks and waysides along Lake Superior's North Shore. Magney believed that "Our state parks are everyone's country estate."

For more information about this park contact: Judge C. R. Magney State Park, Box 500 E. Star Route, Grand Marais, MN 55604. Phones 218–387–2929 and 218–226–3539. See also the address for the DNR Information Center at the front of the book.

Upper Falls, Brule River, Judge C. R. Magney State Park (Greg L. Ryan and Sally A. Beyer)

SPLIT ROCK LIGHTHOUSE

There is an urge within all of us to go to the coast. In Minnesota, our "coast" is the Lake Superior shoreline. One of the landmarks on our coast is a lighthouse, part of a historic complex at Split Rock Lighthouse State Park and perhaps the most spectacular light on the Great Lakes.

Since 1910, the Split Rock Lighthouse has been both a beacon and a landmark. The area became a state park in 1971 and now includes one of the longest shorelines of Lake Superior for public access. A modern visitor center is operated by the Minnesota Historical Society. The lighthouse, a fog signal building, an oil storage house, and three brick residences let the visitor step back to the days of early shipping.

The park has a rich and varied history. Before there was a lighthouse, logging by the Merrill and Ring Lumber Company took place in the park area from 1899 to 1906, and the operation included a short railroad up the river. Pilings from old booms still jut out of the water at the mouth of Split Rock River.

In 1905, a November gale claimed the steamer Edenborn, the tragedy that fueled demand for the lighthouse with its 370,000-candlepower beacon. There was also a fishing village at nearby Little Two Harbors, and the Minnesota Abrasives Company, now known as 3M Company, mined anorthosite at Corundum Point.

Although most visitors stop to tour the historic lighthouse and museum, Split Rock Lighthouse State Park has many other options for recreation. At a new cart-in campground, visitors use carts to take their gear to high quality, secluded locations. Hiking trails connect with the magnificent Superior Hiking Trail, which parallels much of the coast and passes by beautiful waterfalls. There are many other miles of trails with spectacular overlooks of Lake Superior. In winter, cross-country skiing is very popular.

Near Split Rock River is a parking area and a cobblestone beach that is ripe for stone skipping. Often anglers work the bay for lake trout, salmon, and brown trout. The bays are beautiful and secluded, places to contemplate and find solitude. In the spring the surge of incoming waves lifts and cracks the breaking ice and creates a chorus of ice sounds.

South of the lighthouse is an island bay. This island is near the campground and is connected to the mainland by a tombolo, a gravel-covered land bridge that has been created by wave action. The island is pine studded, a scene right out of canoe country.

The lighthouse cliff is part of a sill, an intrusion of volcanic rocks. The sill is part of the earth's Precambrian history and is related to the rocks exposed throughout the area. The Duluth Complex is made up of many intrusive events, hot magma upwelling in cracks and weak areas of the existing volcanic bedrock. The result is a very hard rock that has withstood the ravages of storms and glaciers to give us the beauty of Split Rock Lighthouse State Park.

For more information about this park contact: Split Rock Lighthouse State Park, 2010A Highway 61 E., Two Harbors, MN 55616. Phone 218–226–3065. See also the address for the DNR Information Center at the front of the book.

Split Rock Lighthouse State Park (Bob Firth)

Yellow Lady's Slipper (Cypripedium calceolus) (Paul Sundberg)

Cross-country skier (Paul Wannarka)

64

In Temperance River State Park, travelers must stop and walk a short distance off the road to view the beautiful series of drops and bends that the Temperance River makes through a very narrow, black-walled gorge. The narrow canyon is a series of potholes that have been connected by river erosion. The potholes formed when water-suspended rocks or sand swirled in one spot for a long period of time. Nearby, more potholes were left high and dry as the river found its new and present channel. A trail takes visitors along the edge of the gorge, and interpretive signs provide helpful graphics. Each stop along the gorge hiking trail gives a different perspective of the river.

The Temperance River drains 180 square miles of watershed as it travels twenty-five miles from Brule Lake in the Boundary Waters Canoe Area Wilderness to Lake Superior. The mix of pine, spruce, cedar, and birch trees along the rocky blufftops provides for a variety of birdlife, especially during the spring and fall migrations. For the angler, brook, brown, and rainbow trout are the magnets. The fish have been stocked in the river, and now the brook and brown trout have established natural populations.

Temperance River State Park has two campgrounds. In both, campers are lulled to sleep by the rhythmic whispering of the waves sweeping up and down the rocky shoreline. The breeze off the lake acts as a natural air conditioner.

The most popular hiking trail follows the river, but six miles of trails let you explore both the wet lowlands and dry uplands of this park's 133 acres. In winter, cross-country skiers and snowmobilers can discover the beauty of the park mantled in white. The ski trails also connect with the Cross River Wayside trails.

Temperance River State Park (Bob Firth)

For more information about this park contact: Temperance River State Park, Box 33, Schroeder, MN 55613. Phones 218–663–7476 and 218–226–3539. See also the address for the DNR Information Center at the front of the book.

TETTEGOUCHE

Lake Superior shoreline, Tettegouche State Park (Bob Firth)

For more information about this park contact: Tettegouche State Park, 474 Highway 61 E., Silver Bay, MN 55614. Phone 218–226–3539. See also the address for the DNR Information Center at the front of the book.

In 1979, Baptism River State Park, a highway rest area, and a newly acquired inland area of lakes, ridges, and historic structures were combined to form Tettegouche State Park. The public can enjoy the visitor center's interpretive materials, picnic among the birch trees, or walk to Shovel Point where the large rhyolite sill provides a breathtaking overlook. From the cliff, visitors can view sea arches, sea caves, points, and coves.

Nature lovers will find beauty everywhere. Going inland, hiking trails along the Baptism River provide views of many falls and cascades, including the stately sixty-foot High Falls. A spectacular portion of the Superior Hiking Trail is good for daytime hikes and backpacking. There is a trailhead with many different directions to hike, a campground, and a group camp.

Anglers work the stream for trout and salmon, or walk to one of the four remote inland lakes for northerns or walleye. The walk inland is through semi-mountainous terrain and requires preparation such as a water bottle and food to supplement the hiker. The scenery is worth the effort. The birch-aspen forests of the shore are replaced by maple, yellow birch, basswood, and white spruce farther inland, where you might find the rare black-throated blue warbler. On dry ridges are oaks, and scattered around the lakes are pines.

Geologists find this park a jumble of over twenty lava flows, of diabase dikes, rhyolite and basalt flows, and cobblestone beaches. Historians can explore the Tettegouche Camp, once used by loggers, which passed from the Alger-Smith Company to a private club in Duluth that used the camp for recreation.

THE MISSISSIPPI RIVER VALLEY PARKS

The Mississippi River Valley Parks

Carley

Frontenac

Itasca *(Major Park)*

Lake Bemidji *(Major Park)*

O. L. Kipp

Schoolcraft

Whitewater *(Major Park)*

The great river Mississippi is really a combination of rivers. The upper stretch is full of beaver dams and flows through numerous fishing lakes. It leaves Itasca State Park and flows through Lake Bemidji and Schoolcraft state parks. The second stretch of the Mississippi has a larger flow and connects more communities. Crow Wing, Lindbergh, and Fort Snelling state parks all lie on this second stretch, but because of the role these areas played in the settlement of the state, the parks are included in the history section of this book.

The third stretch begins with the confluence of the Minnesota River. From this point on, the Mississippi River occupies the valley of the glacial River Warren, and the combined waters of the Mississippi, St. Croix, and Minnesota rivers form a navigable stream for commerce and pleasure boaters. Side streams come in from the flat farmlands and carve steep valleys as they descend to the Mississippi. Rivers that flow through Whitewater and Carley state parks are major tributaries in this stretch of the Mississippi. The Upper Mississippi River National Wildlife Refuge protects the wildlife-rich deltas of these streams, while Frontenac and O. L. Kipp state parks protect sensitive uplands.

CARLEY

The approach to Carley State Park is past gently rolling hills of farmland and pasture. The park itself features a diverse forest with a quiet river and streams flowing through the valleys.

The landforms of the area were formed long, long ago. Glacial meltwater fed the streams that cut through the soil and limestone bedrock. Loess (fine-grained silt) was blown southward from the glaciers and deposited here.

Five miles of trails are here for skiers, and almost six miles of trails for hikers. The trails range from moderate climbs up the valley to less strenuous paths that follow the flow of the Whitewater River. For the springtime hiker, the floral display is accentuated by the beautiful sky-blue flowers of Virginia bluebells, uncommon in other parts of the Whitewater valley.

In the picnic grounds, adults and children can play on the swings, pitch horseshoes, play a game of softball, or just sit back and marvel at the majestic beauty of the great old white pines on the steep slope that rises up from the river's edge. The parkland was donated to the state in 1948 by two families in hopes of preserving this native grove of trees. Wooded campsites are scattered above the picnic area.

House wrens, orioles, song sparrows, and indigo buntings are a few of the birds that fill the air with song. Swallowtail butterflies drift lazily above the stream, while black-winged damselflies and water striders feed at the water's surface and crayfish hide under submerged rocks. Overhead a young red-tail hawk rides thermals that rise from the floor of this secluded valley.

For more information about this park contact: Carley State Park, Route 1, Box 256, Altura, MN 55910. Phones 507–534–3400 and 507–932–3007. See also the address for the DNR Information Center at the front of the book.

Virginia Bluebells (Mertensia virginica) *(Joe Niznik)*

Each May, there is a major bird migration north through Frontenac State Park. If the water level on the Mississippi isn't too high, Sand Point is a shorebird and warbler paradise. The scattered woodlands and grasslands on the blufftops always· offer good birdwatching. Around the campground are orchard orioles, rose-breasted grosbeaks, bluebirds, and field sparrows, and along the trails you can expect to find a tremendous variety of birds, including the blue-winged warbler.

The park encompasses bluff, prairie, floodplain forest, and hardwood forest. On both sides of the bluff, the valley is steep-sided and deep. On one side is the Pleasant Valley Creek and marsh-lake complex where one channel of the glacial River Warren once flowed. In post-glacial times, large predecessors of the St. Croix and Minnesota rivers merged to carve the valley of the Mississippi. The bluff was an island at that time.

In more recent history, In Yan Teopa Rock has been a local landmark, and from the picnic area overlook there could have been a view of the town of Frontenac and the furpost. Frontenac was a popular tourist destination in the days of the steamboat, but with the arrival of the railroad, Frontenac slowly became a quiet remnant of a different century. The Frontenac Park Association deserves a lot of credit for the formation of the state park.

Today, tourists can enjoy the natural beauty of this landscape by hiking, skiing, and snowmobiling. The spring flowers and fall colors are specialties of the park.

*Fall color, Sumac (*Rhus sp.*) (Joe Niznik)*

For more information about this park contact: Frontenac State Park, Route 2, Box 134, Lake City, MN 55041. Phone 612-345-3401. See also the address for the DNR Information Center at the front of the book.

ITASCA

Tall stands of virgin pine still shade parts of Itasca State Park. Pristine blue lakes shimmer in the summer sun. Eagles raise their young in massive nests that are supported by ancient pines, and pine duff muffles the sound of footsteps. These stands are cathedrals of the northern forest, quiet groves where lucky summer hikers might view the moccasin flower.

In 1891, a law was passed to establish the boundaries of Itasca, Minnesota's oldest state park and the source of the Mississippi River. Numerous attempts were made to trace the river to its beginning, often at government expense, and the names of the explorers are a mixed roll call of famous and infamous. Even when Henry Schoolcraft declared the waters of Lake Itasca as the source, efforts were still made to go beyond the lake to the source of the lake's smaller tributaries.

Because of the controversy, the Minnesota Historical Society commissioned Jacob Vradenberg Brower to survey and map Itasca. Brower, with the help of twenty-four assistants, spent 160 days over a period of three years completing the project. During his survey, Brower found the towering pine groves and realized that they were more valuable than the naming of the river's source. As a result he devoted his energies to establishing a park and serving as its first superintendent.

For many people, seeing the pines and walking under their spreading boughs are as important as crossing the fledgling Mississippi. One of the most spectacular trails leads to Bohall Lake through a corridor of trees more than two hundred years old. The largest red pine in Minnesota is found on the Big Pine Trail, standing 120 feet tall and more than nine feet in diameter. Not far away grows the largest white pine in the state. Twenty-seven kinds of orchids and a variety of native wildflowers grow throughout the forest.

The park preserves many lakes and a complex mosaic of plant communities. The park also contains a wilderness sanctuary, a two thousand–acre natural area that is considered a state Scientific and Natural Area and a registered National Natural Landmark by the National Park Service.

The history of this park far exceeds Schoolcraft's expedition. Native Americans were living at the lake when the "discovery" was made. Artifacts have been found in the Nicollet Creek area that document the lives of a hunting people who survived on large hoofed animals eight thousand years ago. These hunters were followed by people of the Woodland Period who established more permanent settlements. These people harvested wild rice and tapped maple trees, practices that have survived the passage of centuries. They also hunted big game, but with the development of the bow and arrow, their choice of game increased and success improved, allowing their culture to advance.

Signs of the Native Americans' existence can still be seen within the park boundaries. A bison kill site and burial mounds are in the park. Preserving the human past in Itasca gives us a cultural insight as well as an understanding and appreciation of the natural beauty.

Over five hundred thousand people visit the thirty-two thousand acre park annually to see the waters begin their 2,552-mile journey to the Gulf of Mexico. Most visitors want to skip across the boulder-strewn outlet of the lake to cross the point where the accumulated waters of the basin become a river, but the visitors who get the most satisfaction are those who see the historic log buildings, the fire tower, museums, and pine groves, and participate in the naturalist programs, finding their own special memories.

For more information about this park contact: Itasca State Park, Lake Itasca, MN 56460. Phones 218–266–3654 and 218–266–3656. See also the address for the DNR Information Center at the front of the book.

Itasca State Park (Bob Firth)

Headwaters of the Mississippi River, Itasca State Park (Bob Firth)

Showy Lady's Slipper (Cypripedium reginae) *(Paul Sundberg)*

A trail in Lake Bemidji State Park leads up and over a small rise between oak, birch, and occasional pine trees. At the base of the slope a boardwalk replaces the trail. Tamarack and black spruce take over the canopy, and hyssop and aster on the forest floor are replaced by showy lady's slippers, bog beans, cranberries, and other plants of the bog.

Instead of glacial till, the soil is peat and sphagnum. The ground is not solid, it is spongy and wet. Insect-eating plants, for example, sundew and the pitcher plant, live here; the buzzing sound of warblers and the crisp, clear notes of white-throated sparrows fill this wet woodland.

In spring, this area is full of migrating birds and flowers like Labrador tea and bog bean. The month of June is host to an orchid display, and by July the bog is overwhelmingly green, with a few scattered flowers.

The park is located on a glacial moraine, which gives the landscape a rolling relief. The melting glacier was the park's main architect. Blocks broke off of the decaying ice mass and were buried in glacial debris. When these blocks melted, depressions were left. Small blocks created ponds, marshes, and bogs, and two large blocks were responsible for Lake Bemidji. Meltwater generated a flat outwash that created the picnic area and a sandy beach for today's swimmers.

The lake is part of the Mississippi River, and is one of a chain of lakes in the headwaters including Bemidji, Wolf, Andrusia, and Cass. The waters that flow from Lake Itasca enter Lake Bemidji on the southwest and flow out the east side. The water you swim in here is headed for the Gulf of Mexico, and this is a good place to begin a Mississippi River canoe trip.

From the overlook at Rocky Point the lake spreads out to the south and hikers can observe sailboating, motorboating, and fishing. The lake is a backdrop for the city of Bemidji and many resorts and homes.

The pine forest around Lake Bemidji was home to the Dakota Indians until they were driven out and replaced by the Ojibwe. Lumbermen were attracted to the tall pines and most of the surrounding area was logged. The park protects some remnant virgin timber. Paul Bunyan and Babe the Blue Ox are symbolic of our romantic image of the logger, but the old pines are the real giants.

The southwest quarter of the park is the most heavily used, with campgrounds, a visitor center, a beach, a picnic area, an interpretive trail, a boat ramp and harbor, a winter trail center, a dining hall for groups, and an electrical hook-ups in part of the campground. The visitor center is an excellent place to begin. There, informative displays and naturalist-led activities focus on the park's special qualities.

This park truly sparkles on crisp Minnesota winter days with the beauty of the deep snow, the icy lakes, and the blanketed forests. Snowmobiling and cross-country skiing trails radiate from the heated trail center, and ice fishing is popular on the lake. The park naturalists lead snowshoe hikes and other programs throughout the winter.

For more information about this park contact: Lake Bemidji State Park, 3401 State Park Road NE, Bemidji, MN 56601. Phone 218-755-3843. See also the address for the DNR Information Center at the front of the book.

Bog boardwalk, Lake Bemidji State Park (Minnesota DNR)

*Pitcher Plant (*Sarracenia purpurea*)*
(Greg L. Ryan and Sally A. Beyer)

*Great Blue Heron (*Ardea herodias) *(Walt Huss)*

O. L. KIPP

Queen's Bluff, O. L. Kipp State Park (Joe Niznik/Minnesota DNR)

This park is a "natural" state park, which emphasizes the protection and restoration of its natural resources. The park is a landscape for hiking, nature study, and skiing, with breathtaking overlooks. The picnic tables are shielded from one another and the campground is nestled in among tall sumac and hardwoods.

In general, the park can be described as a combination of hardwoods, pine plantations, prairie, and old fields, but naturalists can explore each of these areas and find a great deal of diversity. North facing slopes are cool and damp, south facing slopes are hot and dry, and there are lots of variations in between.

A white cedar community, a natural for northeastern Minnesota, is left over from the days of the glaciers. On steep (forty- to fifty-degree), south-southwest facing slopes are "goat prairies," unique to southeastern Minnesota.

Queen's Bluff and King's Bluff are Scientific and Natural Areas. They are limestone-capped with little bluestem, side-oats grama, compass plant, lead plant, silky aster, and blazing star among the prairie mix.

The wildlife includes wild turkeys and ruffed grouse, six-lined racers (a lizard), timber rattlesnakes, opossums, coyotes, spotted skunks, and indigo buntings. In the old fields some spectacular birding can be done. The bobolink sings a bubbly aerial song and the Henslow's sparrow issues an inconspicuous call—"Tslick." Birdwatchers flock here for this hard-to-find species.

For more information about this park contact: O. L. Kipp State Park, Route 4, Winona, MN 55987. Phone 507-643-6849. See also the address for the DNR Information Center at the front of the book.

Schoolcraft State Park's interpretive trail is called the Whisper Trail. That is a good theme for the entire park, a 295-acre beauty. The trail leads through the virgin pine forest, a cathedrallike grove of conifers. One white pine is over three hundred years old. Light filters through the branches of red pine, white pine, jack pine, spruce, and fir trees. Bird songs are muted by the overstory and footsteps are muffled by the spongy carpet of pine needles.

Henry Rowe Schoolcraft not only established the location of the Mississippi headwaters, but as a Native American agent for the region, he also collected local myths. This quiet park on the shore of the Mississippi embodies the spirits of both forest and river and honors both Schoolcraft and the natives who lived here.

Here, the Mississippi River is small and ideal for canoeing but large enough for other craft. The current is steady. There are large areas of wild rice, beds of yellow and white water lilies, and a mix of open sloughs, phragmites, and sedge marsh. There is an oxbow lake in the marsh near the Vermilion River. This is an old channel that was separated by alluvial deposits and a dynamic river system.

The park has a boat access, picnic area, campground, and twelve canoe campsites. The campgrounds usually have vacancies but can fill up during duck hunting season and the early part of fishing season. The Forest History Center near Grand Rapids is a good place to visit when staying at Schoolcraft State Park.

Most of the year the park offers solitude to visitors, with only the whisper of the wind through the pines to accompany their thoughts.

Mississippi River, Schoolcraft State Park (Carmelita McGurk/Minnesota DNR)

For more information about this park contact: Schoolcraft State Park, HCR 4, Box 181, Deer River, MN 56636. Phone 218–566–2383. See also the address for the DNR Information Center at the front of the book.

WHITEWATER

Most parks stand out from their surroundings. Many are reminiscent of the landscape before it was settled, and the surrounding countryside is a sharp contrast with the park. That is not the way it is at Whitewater State Park, where the park and the adjacent Whitewater Wildlife Management Area are the culmination of a restoration project that included the entire valley.

The Whitewater River was named by the Native Americans who enjoyed the lively stream that turns white in the spring as it erodes light-colored clay deposits. The stream flows through the park, the wildlife management area, and the heart of the Richard J. Dorer Memorial Hardwood Forest. In the river valley, there are tall bluffs with limestone cliffs, deep ravines, steep goat prairies, river floodplain forests, and waterfowl pools.

The wildflower-carpeted slopes haven't always been covered with vegetation. The hardwoods weren't always healthy and diverse. After an 1851 treaty with the Dakota Indians, the valley opened up to agriculture and settlement by white emigrants. The settlers cleared the natural vegetation off the hillsides and planted the lowlands. Grazing livestock trampled the native plants, and rainwater cut gullies in the pastures.

Erosion and flooding became serious problems. Nineteen thirty-eight was the worst year: Storms raged and water rolled down the steep slopes, carrying huge loads of topsoil. The side streams were swollen and the Whitewater River pushed a wall of water that ravaged the bottomlands. The former town of Beaver, eight miles north of the park, was flooded twenty-eight times. Today, Beaver is buried beneath several feet of sediment.

Luckily, one of Minnesota's conservation leaders entered the valley and saw the future instead of the destruction. Richard Dorer envisioned a valley that combined people and nature in harmony. He saw conservation and recreation. Now visitors see a land of natural beauty and diversity. Golden eagles winter in the valley, Louisiana waterthrushes nest along the stream banks. This is the valley where the wild turkey was re-established in 1964. Timber rattlesnakes are found here, but few visitors will be lucky enough to glimpse one in the wild. The visitor center, which emphasizes the natural history of the entire valley, has a rattlesnake on exhibit.

In the valley you'll find mixed hardwoods, floodplain forests, and wetlands—a great variety of plants and animals, many that are not found elsewhere in Minnesota. These resources, combined with the valley's land use history, give the park's year-round naturalist many exciting stories to share with visitors through displays and programming.

Numerous trails lead up, around, and over the bluffs. In the spring, these trails offer impressive hillside floral displays, and in the summer the trails are shaded by lush vegetation. The Whitewater River is fed by springs from the Jordan sandstone in the area, and the coolness of the water helps to keep the streamside trails a bit cooler in the summer.

This is southern Minnesota's busiest park, offering a rich variety of activities for nature enthusiasts as well as families of picnickers. The popular swimming beach is along an oxbow lake fed by the clear, spring-fed stream. A picnic shelter and two picnic grounds are liberally shaded by hardwoods. Anglers can try for brown trout or seek the hideaways for rainbows and brookies.

Some people come here for only a day, but there are lots of options for longer stays: the modern campground, walk-in campsites, a primitive group camp, and a modern group center with winterized cabins. One attraction of this park is that because of little standing water there are very few breeding areas for mosquitoes, providing visitors with an almost mosquito-free park experience.

For more information about this park contact: Whitewater State Park, Route 1, Box 256, Altura, MN 55910. Phone 507–932–3007. See also the address for the DNR Information Center at the front of the book.

View from Inspiration Point, Whitewater State Park (Greg L. Ryan and Sally A. Beyer)

Coyote Point, Whitewater State Park (Dave Palmquist)

*Rue Anemone (*Anemonella thalictroides)
(Greg L. Ryan and Sally A. Beyer)

THE ST. CROIX RIVER AND TRIBUTARIES PARKS

The St. Croix River and Tributaries Parks

Afton
Banning *(Hidden Gem)*
Interstate *(Major Park)*
St. Croix *(Major Park)*
Wild River
William O'Brien *(Major Park)*

The St. Croix is both a popular canoe river and a major recreation valley. Five parks, plus Banning State Park on the Kettle River, help tourists and residents explore these woodlands and rivers.

The Kettle River was formed by the drainage for the Nemadji stage of glacial Lake Duluth. The St. Croix drained a later stage of glacial Lake Duluth and glacial Lake Grantsburg.

Today, the St. Croix flows through exposures of volcanic rock and a combination of younger sedimentary beds and through rapids at St. Croix and Interstate state parks. The Kettle has rapids scattered along its entire course and flows through Hell's Gate Canyon at Banning State Park. The Kettle also has a series of rapids as it ends its course on the boundary of St. Croix State Park.

Many of the numerous islands in the St. Croix River are protected by St. Croix State Park. William O'Brien and Afton state parks are very close to the Twin Cities and provide convenient escapes for area residents.

All these parks are natural areas that emphasize trails, boating, and exploration. The Minnesota–Wisconsin Boundary Corridor Trail goes through Wild River and St. Croix state parks. Chengwatana and St. Croix state forests add to the valley's public lands. The St. Croix is one of the original eight rivers in the National Wild and Scenic River program, and the Kettle and Snake rivers are part of the state's Wild and Scenic River program.

AFTON

Afton State Park is a backpacker's park, a picnic area, and a nature preserve all within an hour's drive of two and a half million residents of the Twin Cities area. The park's beauty is a good example of why the lower St. Croix was designated a National Scenic River.

Set in rolling glacial moraine and blufflands, the landscape is a combination of natural grasslands and woodlands. The forests are a combination of ravine hardwoods and pine plantations. Remnant prairies are being expanded and oak savannas are being restored through an aggressive resource management program.

Established in 1969, the park was designed to provide recreational opportunities for the metropolitan area and to preserve the special qualities of the river blufflands. Afton State Park has a visitor center (an indoor picnic shelter), a swimming beach on the St. Croix, and paved and backcountry trails. There are also twenty-four backpack campsites, a canoe campsite, and two group camps.

Afton is wonderfully suited for hiking and has challenging cross-country ski trails. Birdwatchers can observe hawks and ducks on the St. Croix flyway, bluebirds in the grasslands, and waves of migratory birds in the floodplains. Deer, fox, and badgers live here, along with the thirteen-lined ground squirrel, gray, and fox squirrels.

The floral display progresses from pasqueflowers and woodland ephemerals in the spring, to the butterfly weed and puccoons on the summer prairie, and finally to fall's sunflowers and blazing stars.

Forget the closeness of the city. The sounds of a bubbling brook and the songs of bluebirds and meadowlarks are the right music for these surroundings.

For more information about this park contact: Afton State Park, 6959 Peller Ave S., Hastings, MN 55033. Phone 612-436-5391. See also the address for the DNR Information Center at the front of the book.

Afton State Park (Greg L. Ryan and Sally A. Beyer)

Banning State Park is a silent sentinel for past dreams of stagecoaches and railroad steam engines along the banks of a singing river. Here, men carved great sandstone blocks for distant cities and named their community Banning after a railroad official who would never set foot in the town. The town was short lived, doomed by the great Hinckley fire of 1894 and the then-new use of steel girders in the building industry. Banning State Park has an abandoned quarry with ochre-stained walls in midst of a sandstone valley.

A not-so-silent stream sings songs of another type of dream — river dreams. Plastic kayaks bob in the swollen waters, playing in souse-holes and rapids. Paddlers dare the energies of Blueberry Slide, Mother's Delight, Dragon Tooth, Ghost-town Rapids, and Hell's Gate. Canoes float the rapids in low water levels, and hikers explore the mossy shoreline rocks.

Banning State Park is a remote and unique beauty. Rock outcrops laced with polypody fern mark old river shorelines. An old channel of the glacial Kettle River is now a forest area of cliffs. Sandstone dominates the park with bands of color that paint geologic stories of a Precambrian lake that extended south to Kansas. Now, water seeps through the cracks of the stone cliffs along the river's edge, supporting the rare bird's-eye primrose and creating ice falls in the winter.

On Log Drive Creek, a large natural arch stands out from one of the valley walls. Smaller erosional formations line the river beneath the canoe campsite at Rock Dam. This was a ford for crossing the river in the 1800s.

The songs of the scarlet tanager and the ovenbird reverberate in the woods that encompass the old travel routes. Aspen and birch forests that followed the great fire of 1894 now shade the trackless railroad grades, while conifers grow along the river route of the XY and Northwest Company fur traders.

Highway 61 traverses one park boundary, the major road before freeway travel. The oldest reminders of wheeled travel are the patches of roadway that carried stage coaches from Point Douglas (near the mouth of the St. Croix River) to Superior, Wisconsin, in the middle to late 1800s. Known as the "Military Road," it is a significant path through time and nature; a kiosk in the park commemorates the old roadway.

Banning is a park to wander in, with the secluded Wolf Creek rapids and falls hidden in the woods, smooth-walled kettles in the valleys, steep ski trails, and easily traversed old railroad beds for walking and skiing. A snowmobile trail, a campground, picnic grounds, and a boat landing provide all the services that this nature-oriented park needs.

For more information about this park contact: Banning State Park, P.O. Box 643, Sandstone, MN 55072. Phone 612–245–2668. See also the address for the DNR Information Center at the front of the book.

Hell's Gate Rapids, Kettle River, Banning State Park (Randy Gordon)

Wolf Creek Falls, Banning State Park (Walt Huss)

Paper Birch (Betula papyrifera), *Kettle River*
(Greg L. Ryan and Sally A. Beyer)

85

INTERSTATE

Minnesota claims the world's deepest potholes — as deep as sixty feet. The large holes, near the town of Taylors Falls and part of the geologic maze of Interstate State Park, were carved ten thousand years ago by a raging river that drained glacial Lakes Grantsburg and Duluth.

Water roars in the dalles of the St. Croix River where dark volcanic rocks form the flat walls of the canyon. The water rushes through the constriction in a swirling mass of boils, waves, and eddies. At the end of the Pleistocene Epoch, the scene would have been similar, but the turbulence was at a higher elevation and the water volume was 140 to 200 times greater. In the eddies, sand and loose rocks were swirled and spun over the bedrock with enough energy to drill holes into the rock, forming today's potholes.

Geologists find the area around Interstate State Park a classic showcase of North American geology. There, they count seven to ten lava flows, find two distinct glacial deposits, and trace a complex system of old stream valleys and faults. Highway 8 descends into the St. Croix River valley through a sequence of rock layers that records the history of ancient seabeds. The Cambrian seas washed the basaltic lavas, leaving marine fossils in shoreline conglomerates and some sediment beds.

By the time the waterfalls above the gorge were dammed (in 1906), the gorge had seen Native American and voyageur canoes, regular steamboat traffic, and log jams of legendary proportions. There were speculative copper mining ventures and milling, but the communities in Minnesota and Wisconsin were primarily gateways for the exploitation of white pine forests. Stagecoach lines, railroad tracks, and highways have cut through the park and have carried both adventurers and tourists. The Folsom House and buildings on Angel Hill represent the development and wealth of Taylors Falls's boom years.

Visitors can kayak in the rapids beneath the bridge, canoe the flatwater, climb the cliffs, picnic near the boat launch, or explore the park's geology and history with the summer naturalist program. They can hike back to Curtain Falls, past the foundations of a railroad trestle, and enter into a steep valley beneath sedimentary cliffs. A small waterfall plunges over a horseshoe-shaped amphitheater that is left from the erosion of glacial runoff.

The river is a migratory path for many birds, and offers habitat for northerns, walleye, smallmouth bass, and numerous other species. It is also habitat for over forty species of mussels, many of which are in danger of extinction elsewhere. The forest is a mix of floodplain, upland hardwoods, and conifer stands.

On the other side of the St. Croix, Wisconsin offers a companion park and many different services. Together, the two parks protect a geologically significant area.

For more information about this park contact: Interstate State Park, Box 254, Taylors Falls, MN 55084. Phone 612–465–5711. See also the address for the DNR Information Center at the front of the book.

Kayaker, St. Croix River (Bob Firth)

The Bake Oven Pothole, Interstate State Park (Joe Niznik)

St. Croix River (Joe Niznik)

Rivers make this park special. The St. Croix is one of the original eight National Wild and Scenic Rivers, and the Kettle River, which parallels the western boundary of St. Croix State Park, is the first Minnesota State Wild and Scenic River. Both are great rivers to canoe with a combination of rapids and flatwater. Both rivers were historic riverways for the XY and Northwest Fur companies, the Dakota and the Ojibwe Indians, explorers, and loggers. There is outstanding bass fishing in the St. Croix, and good walleye, smallmouth bass, and sauger fishing in the Kettle.

Lesser known areas in the park include the Sand River, Hay Creek, and Crooked Creek. The Sand River provides a pleasant canoe ride from where the river crosses the park road to its mouth on the St. Croix. Hay Creek is a good trout stream; an impoundment turns part of the creek into Lake Clayton, the site of the park's swimming beach. Crooked Creek is on the northeast side and has a walk-in camp area for backcountry explorers.

Of the over 250 islands in the St. Croix River channel, one-fourth are in this park. They range from teardrop sand islands that are slowly migrating downstream with the current, to large bedrock anchored islands that divide the St. Croix into two rivers from Bear Creek to the Kettle River.

Over 125 miles of hiking trails, seventy-five miles of horseback trails, a bicycle trail, primitive roads, snowmobile trails, and cross-country ski trails help visitors explore the thirty-four thousand acres of woodlands. More than a short visit is required to get the real essence of this country.

A variety of campsite types provides visitors with modern conveniences and backcountry experiences: canoe campsites, walk-in campsites, drive-in campsites, a large primitive group camp, modern group centers, and horseback riding campsites.

Deer are abundant at this park, and in the evening they are very easy to see. Grouse are common along the roads. Coyotes, rabbits, foxes, chipmunks, squirrels, and even an occasional bear can be part of the park experience. Waves of warblers follow the river in migrations, and eagles and osprey are common along the St. Croix. The woodcock dances near the alder swamps, the kingfisher forages along the stream banks, and the great blue heron searches for frogs in the slow waters.

From the firetower lookout a diversity of wet and upland plant communities can be seen. There are riverine communities, lowland ash swamps, and upland woodlands. Prairie plants grow on the uplands, and a newer successional forest grows where a straight-line windstorm disturbed the uniformity of growth.

There is very little evidence of the Native American villages and the fur post that were in the park, but St. John's Landing is named for a logging camp operator, and the base camp is still used by groups, and portions of the old Fleming Railroad are now incorporated into the park entrance road. The railroad ended at Big Yellow Banks where its load of logs was discharged into the river to float downstream to the mills.

For more information about this park contact: St. Croix State Park, Route 3, Box 450, Hinckley, MN 55037. Phones 612–384–6591 and 612–384–6657. See also the address for the DNR Information Center at the front of the book.

Trail along the Kettle River, St. Croix River State Park (Alan Jueneman)

St. Croix River (Bob Firth)

90

Beaver (Castor canadensis) *(Dominique Braud)*

WILD RIVER

Wild River State Park is a long, narrow park that protects twenty miles of the St. Croix River valley from development. The park's northern border begins at Chengwatana State Forest, and the river offers canoers an outstanding scenic float as well as canoe campsites. Canoe rentals and shuttles are available in the park. The stretch of river from Sunrise Landing to the southern park landing is popular for day trips.

The Sunrise River, a second wild river for the park, plunges into the St. Croix. This river is smaller than the St. Croix, with abundant wildlife and riffles, and provides habitat for beaver, waterfowl, and songbirds.

The rivers and abundant wildlife attracted early fur traders. The park includes the sites of two historic furposts: the Maurice Samuels Post, located here in 1846, and Thomas Connor's Goose Creek Post, built in 1847. People passed through this park on a stagecoach road that began near the mouth of the St. Croix River and ended at Lake Superior, on the Arrow Line Railroad, and aboard a river ferry.

The river powered a sawmill and a gristmill, and floated the white pine logs that were being harvested from the forests. Nevers Dam on the St. Croix was the world's largest wooden, pile-driven dam and is one of the park's most significant historic sites. The water that swirls around the remaining pilings creates currents that can be dangerous and visitors should not swim here.

A complex of floodplain wetlands, sand plain oaks and conifers, riverine hardwoods, and scattered prairies provide habitat for black bears, nesting bald eagles, otters, coyotes, and foxes, and great recreational opportunities for hikers, horseback riders, skiers, and campers.

A trail center, visitor center, park naturalist

Wild River State Park Trail Center (Carmelita McGurk/Minnesota DNR)

program, winterized shower building, and nature trail all add to the pleasure of the park experience.

For more information about this park contact: Wild River State Park, 39755 Park Trail, Center City, MN 55012. Phone 612–583–2125. See also the address for the DNR Information Center at the front of the book.

Only one hour from the Twin Cities metropolitan area, William O'Brien provides quality recreation and a beautiful natural environment for a large urban population. Yet the park still maintains opportunities for those who like to "get away" for solitude and reflection. The park is located on the St. Croix River, and the river's wooded islands, deep valley, and natural migratory pathway all provide the paddler, picnicker, skier, naturalist, and angler with great diversity.

The picnic grounds and beach are popular with families; the channels of the St. Croix have northerns, walleye, bass, and trout; the birds that follow the river scatter in the diverse plant communities. Explorers find a lake, marshes, and meadows, and maple-basswood, oak-hickory, floodplain, and pine forests. Hawks put on spectacular displays in the spring and fall, and warblers move through the forest in bursts of color and activity.

Wildflowers give color to the spring woods and the summer fields. Hawks soar above the meadows and lightning bugs flicker in the night. Greenberg Island is visible from the picnic grounds, but accessible only by boat. This helps to protect the island and to keep it a wildlife and wildflower sanctuary.

Canoe concessions, refreshment stands, and a visitor center provide an assortment of options. A paved bike trail extends beyond the park, and paved trails can be used for wheelchairs. The trails across the highway from the river are on rolling country, ideal for hiking in summer and skiing in winter. The park also serves as a river access for those who want to travel the historic voyageur and logging routes.

Unlike much of the St. Croix valley, this parkland was oak savanna and prairie. William

O'Brien was a lumber baron who bought up much of the land that had been cut over. In 1945, his daughter Alice donated 180 acres to be developed into a park. It has since grown to 1,353 acres.

The farmers arrived after the loggers, and the first Swedish community in the state was formed in Scandia, just north of the park. Wilder Forest, a convention center and natural area; the St. Croix Islands, which are managed by the National Park Service; and Square Lake, a regional park, are other recreational sites for those who want to camp at William O'Brien and explore the area.

For more information about this park contact: William O'Brien State Park, 16821 O'Brien Trail N., Marine on St. Croix, MN 55047. Phone 612-433-2421. See also the address for the DNR Information Center at the front of the book.

Interpreter, William O'Brien State Park
(Judy Thompson/Minnesota DNR)

White-tailed Deer (Odocoileus virginianus) *(Dominique Braud)*

Canoeists, St. Croix River
(Tim Smalley/Minnesota DNR)

THE MINNESOTA RIVER VALLEY PARKS

The Minnesota River valley rivals the Mississippi River valley and North Shore areas as a scenic vacation route. In addition to the five natural history parks that are featured in this section of the book, the Minnesota River valley is host to three parks that are featured in the history section.

From Big Stone Lake near the source of the river to Fort Snelling at its mouth, the Minnesota River combines history with dramatic bluffs. The river flows through the broad, deep valley of the glacial River Warren, which was created by the drainage of glacial Lake Agassiz at the end of the glacial period.

The parks' emphases range from the boat access orientation of Big Stone Lake to the complex trail systems of Minnesota Valley State Park. Flandrau, Minneopa, Lac qui Parle, and Upper Sioux Agency all protect part of a tributary to the Minnesota. Only Minneopa has a waterfall.

In the western half of the river valley, gneiss, one of the planet's oldest rocks, is exposed. In the eastern half, the bedrock is younger limestone, shale, and sandstone.

Wildlife is abundant in the valley, and Big Stone Wildlife Refuge and Lac qui Parle Wildlife Management Area protect western waterfowl areas, while the Minnesota River Valley National Wildlife Refuge protects the floodplain near the mouth of the river. The state parks extend protection to critical wildlife habitat.

The Minnesota River Valley Parks
Big Stone Lake
Flandrau
Lac qui Parle
Minneopa
Minnesota Valley

Big Stone Lake, on the Dakota-Minnesota border, is a body of water thirty miles long and the source of the Minnesota River. Long ago, this area was the south end of glacial Lake Agassiz, once the world's largest freshwater lake, which drained and helped carve the present valley of the Minnesota River.

The park is divided into two units, Meadowbrook and Bonanza, both with boat launch and picnic areas. The shorelines are wooded with large cottonwoods, ashes, and silver maples. The Meadowbrook area has a campground as well as hiking trails. The grasslands in the Meadowbrook area are predominantly old field forbs. Thirty acres of the northern Bonanza unit comprise a rare glacial till hill prairie. The prairie had been grazed, but is now close to presettlement plant composition.

Meadowlarks sing in the dry fields, sedge wrens call from the wet fields, and robins, thrashers, and mourning doves are active in the picnic and camp areas. Deer use the area especially for winter food, and fat little thirteen-lined ground squirrels scurry around in the mowed grass.

Most park users are anxious to get on the lake to do some angling. Walleye are the primary game fish, but there are also some big perch, northerns, and bluegills. The park includes northern- and bluegill-rearing ponds. In the winter, ice fishing and ice boating are two ways to beat the cold.

Big Stone Lake State Park (Keith Wendt/Minnesota DNR)

For more information about this park contact: Big Stone Lake State Park, Route 1, Box 153, Ortonville, MN 56278. Phone 612–839–3663. See also the address for the DNR Information Center at the front of the book.

FLANDRAU

Flandrau is a state park that is enjoyed by many of the local citizens of New Ulm. Part of its border lies within the city of New Ulm. The picnic grounds and swimming area attract the crowds, both travelers and locals, but it would be a mistake not to look beyond this busy section of the park.

This park encompasses a portion of the Cottonwood River, and the cottonwoods that grow along the banks are among the largest trees in the area. A nature trail helps explain the environment around the river. Wood ducks, kingfishers, and other birds can be heard along this gently flowing river. The south side of the park has no trails and is protected from overuse as a result. Stream erosion has exposed sandstone and conglomerate rock that were laid down long ago in a lagoon of an ancient sea.

Joggers, walkers, and skiers can get exercise and a good look at the diverse scenery with a choice between flat trails in the bottom of the Cottonwood River valley or steeper routes up the hillsides. The hilltops offer vistas of the interesting hill prairie. This park is also good for viewing wildlife, especially deer in the early morning or early evening. The campgrounds are shaded by large deciduous trees and several nice black walnut trees. There are also two group camps.

Neighboring New Ulm has a rich immigrant history, adding a strong German accent to the community. In addition, major battles in the U.S.–Dakota Conflict of 1862 were fought in the area, although none were fought in the park itself. The park was later named in honor of Charles Flandrau, an attorney and Native American agent who organized a group of volunteers to protect New Ulm during the siege.

The historic stone buildings in the park are fine examples of rustic architecture crafted by the WPA. The WPA also built a major dam in the park, and the CCC built trails and planted trees. The modern group camp in the park once served as a CCC camp and a German prisoner of war camp. Today, it is a happier gathering place for youth groups and other organizations.

For more information about this park contact: Flandrau State Park, 1300 Summit Ave, New Ulm, MN 56073. Phone 507–354–3519. See also the address for the DNR Information Center at the front of the book.

Cottonwood River, Flandrau State Park (Bill Rooks)

Lac qui Parle Wildlife Management Area extends along thirteen miles of river edge and lakeshore and surrounds the state park. The lake is one mile wide and only fourteen feet deep, so the area contains lots of wildlife habitat. Pelicans, herons, terns, gulls, and shorebirds are found along the entire length of the lake, and the park is a good viewing spot. The refuge is known for its goose management; spring and fall migrations can be spectacular.

A canoe landing puts paddlers into the Lac qui Parle River; a boat landing is available on the lake. Anglers can try for walleye, northerns, perch, or crappie, or simply observe the wildlife. Catfish can be caught in the Minnesota River, below the Lac qui Parle dam.

The picnic area and campgrounds have an abundance of wildlife too. Deer are seen regularly, as are gray squirrels and ground squirrels. House wrens like the brushy shoreline. Orioles, catbirds, and robins like the same areas where people concentrate.

The swimming beach has coarse sand surrounding outcrops of gneiss, a granite that is one of the world's oldest rocks. The horse camp, walk-in group camping sites, tent camping area, and modern campgrounds are located on the delta deposits of the Lac qui Parle River. The river carried erosional mud, sand, and gravel that were deposited as the river dropped into the Minnesota River valley and hit the larger and slower Minnesota River. At one time, this delta constricted the larger river's course and backed up water, creating the shallow Lac qui Parle Lake. A flood control dam now controls the lake and its water level.

For more information about this park contact: Lac qui Parle State Park, Route 5, Box 74A, Montevideo, MN 56265. Phone 612–752–4736. See also the address for the DNR Information Center at the front of the book.

Sunrise, Lac qui Parle State Park
(Greg L. Ryan and Sally A. Beyer)

MINNEOPA

The waterfalls of Minneopa Creek are Minneopa State Park's most famous asset. In two steps the water plunges forty-five feet. This portion of the park, near the falls, had groups of up to five thousand that enjoyed picnics as far back as the 1870s, when a small town and depot provided for the tourists' needs. Bridges and paths were established for the celebrants. Then, grasshopper plagues came and destroyed the crops, economy, and community. The park still provides enough picnic tables to accommodate large groups, and a trail allows for leisurely after-dinner strolls along the creek.

On a bedrock river terrace that once abutted the glacial River Warren, a prairie supports bobolinks, bluebirds, and nesting loggerhead shrikes. The grass waves in the breeze and tall stalks of mullein stand as if they were saguaro cacti in the desert. The soil is very thin here and glacial erratics (large boulders) dot the landscape. The campground is set in tall shade-producing trees, and overlooks the Minnesota River.

The Seppmann Windmill is perched just above this terrace. Albert Seppmann used native stone and cut local trees to construct this German-style mill, then had to learn how to use the windmill by trial and error.

For more information about this park contact: Minneopa State Park, Route 9, Box 143, Mankato, MN 56001. Phone 507–625–4388. See also the address for the DNR Information Center at the front of the book.

Historic Seppmann Windmill, Minneopa State Park (Bill Rooks)

The historic, scenic, and recreational opportunities of the lower Minnesota River valley's refuges and park units are tied together by a network of biking, horseback riding, hiking, and snowmobile trails. In its entirety, Minnesota Valley Trail will lead the very ambitious all the way from Fort Snelling to Le Seuer, nearly seventy-five miles. The preservation of this corridor will also enhance the value of a river float trip and protect diverse plant and animal communities.

The deep valley ranges from blufftop oak savannas to river bottom cottonwoods. The ravine plunges up to three hundred feet deep and is five miles wide. Raccoons, mink, muskrat, wood duck, and beaver are some of the animals that require the protection of combined terrestrial-aquatic habitats.

Louisville Swamp, part of a National Wildlife Refuge, is included in the system and features a giant erratic (glacial boulder), an old homestead, bedrock exposure, and wetland that is well known for its bird life. In the grasslands watch for bluebirds, lark sparrows, and migrating loggerhead shrikes. The Carver Rapids unit is also found in this section. Named for Jonathon Carver, the explorer and writer, this is the only rapids in the lower stretch of the river.

Campgrounds and picnic areas are available near the headquarters in the Lawrence unit. The Rush River unit near Le Seuer has a woodland picnic area; Gifford Lake near Chaska is good for fishing. The Chaska-Shakopee bike trail is paved and crosses the river on an old railroad swing bridge. There are canoe and walk-in campsites, and hunting is allowed in some areas.

Special events for hunting dogs, horseback endurance rides, and a sled dog race are part of the activities that make this park very special.

For more information about this park contact: Minnesota Valley State Park, 19825 Park Boulevard, Jordan, MN 55352. Phone 612-492-6400. See also the address for the DNR Information Center at the front of the book.

Sand Creek, Minnesota Valley State Park (Joe Niznik)

THE HISTORICAL PARKS

Minnesota's history is as varied as its landscape. Lake Superior is our inland sea, with freight vessels that have ranged from the Montreal canoe of the voyageurs to the huge vessels that visit Duluth's harbor today. Inland portages are marked by Jay Cooke and Savanna Portage state parks; Split Rock Lighthouse has been a beacon to shipping.

Native American heritage combines later Dakota and Ojibwe history with earlier copper and pottery cultures at Mille Lacs Kathio State Park. Blue Mounds State Park complements Pipestone National Monument and Jeffers Petroglyphs. Crow Wing State Park combines Native American and voyageur history with the story of a town, settlement, and overland trails.

The conflict between the Dakota Indians and early settlers occurred in the areas of Upper Sioux Agency, Fort Ridgely, Lake Shetek, and Monson Lake state parks. Fort Snelling was not directly involved in any conflicts, but marks the beginning of the Twin Cities's story.

Forestville, Camden, Minneopa, Frontenac, Old Mill, and Lake Louise state parks are a mixture of mills, stores, and pioneer dreams in wooded valleys. Banning State Park is the story of mining, a community, and a great forest fire. Other mining stories are found in the Hill Annex and Soudan Underground mines. These two parks are part of the state's famous iron range. The mines were important to our effort in World War I and World War II and were major influences on ethnic migrations.

The story of logging is found in most of the parks but may be strongest at Interstate, Wild River, and St. Croix state parks. In addition, our political and philosophical heritage is represented at Charles A. Lindbergh State Park.

The Historical Parks

Charles A. Lindbergh

Crow Wing

Forestville/Mystery Cave
  (Hidden Gem)

Fort Ridgely

Fort Snelling *(Major Park)*

Hill Annex Mine

Mille Lacs Kathio

Old Mill

Savanna Portage

Soudan Underground Mine
  (Hidden Gem)

Upper Sioux Agency

Located on the Mississippi River, this park honors Charles A. Lindbergh Sr. rather than his famous son. But who can ignore the presence of Charles Lindbergh Jr., the first man to fly solo over the Atlantic, inventor of the heart pump, victim of America's most infamous kidnapping, and one of the world's greatest environmentalists?

Father and son: both leaders, both shapers of today's world. Where would we be today without Charles Sr.'s work in politics? He gave Minnesota the populist voice, was for ten years a Republican congressman, ran for governor with the support of the Nonpartisan League, and became a forerunner in the Farmer-Labor party.

The ultimate tribute to the Lindberghs may not be the plane and the heart pump in the Smithsonian Institution, but rather the preservation of this simple childhood home and the woods, streams, and river valley that spawned so many ideas. The Mississippi River was not dammed when Charles Jr. lived here. He would wade and swim across it, or float the river on a raft or a homemade boat.

Bateaux and wanigans of the lumberjacks came by twice a year, and young Charles joined them for a few meals and watched them log roll and rollick. Of those days he wrote, "My freedom was complete. All he [Charles Sr.] asked for was responsibility in return."

The park includes Pike Creek and a museum (the house Charles Sr. built in 1906), which is operated by the Minnesota Historical Society. There are some beautiful white and red pine stands, as well as aspen and oak. A stone water tower and a couple of log buildings were built in the late 1930s by the WPA. Bald eagles are common sights in spring and fall; the spring wild-

Charles A. Lindbergh House (Connie Wanner)

flowers, fall colors, and winter snows make camping, hiking, skiing, and boating memorable experiences.

Charles Lindbergh Jr. wrote, "Let us never forget that wildness has developed life, including the human species. By comparison, our own accomplishments are trivial."

For more information about this park contact: Charles A. Lindbergh State Park, P.O. Box 364, Little Falls, MN 56345. Phone 612–632–9050. See also the address for the DNR Information Center at the front of the book.

CROW WING

History blends with nature at the confluence of the Mississippi and Crow Wing rivers. Where the rivers meet, the sediment carried by the Crow Wing River has been shaped into an island that Native Americans said looked like a raven's wing. The name "Raven's Wing" was altered to "Crow Wing" and became the name of a river, village, and state park.

Natives, voyageurs, and loggers all used the Crow Wing River for transportation. Another travel route, the Woods Trail, served ox cart traffic that carried supplies between St. Paul and the Red River settlements of Selkirk and Pembina. The park preserves one of the last remaining sections of this twisting, rutted trail. The ox cart trains were made up of eighty to ninety carts and were broken down into brigades of ten, covering twenty miles a day at a rate of two miles per hour. Without lubrication, these wooden carts made an ear piercing din when they moved.

Not all the people traveled past this spot; some decided to stay. An important fur post, built in 1823, took care of French, English, and American fur interests. Catholic, Episcopalian, and Lutheran missions were established here. By the late 1850s, Crow Wing was a bustling, colorful frontier town of over six hundred people. The town of Crow Wing, located on a meander of the Mississippi, died when the railroad chose to cross the Mississippi at the present site of Brainerd. The ferry shut down, and the woods moved in. Interpretive signs and handouts now tell the story of the old town.

Today, visitors come to learn about history, camp in the semi-modern campgrounds, canoe, walk, ski, snowmobile, and fish. The nature lover enjoys the variety of trees: Forty-three of Minnesota's forty-eight species can be found in the park.

For more information about this park contact: Crow Wing State Park, 7100 State Park Road SW, Brainerd, MN 56401. Phone 218–829–8022. See also the address for the DNR Information Center at the front of the book.

Crow River lookout, Crow Wing State Park
(Dan Wennberg/Firth Photobank)

FORESTVILLE/MYSTERY CAVE

Forestville State Park has the distinction of offering visitors beautiful sights both above and below ground. With the 1988 acquisition of Mystery Cave, twelve miles of underground routes were added to the variety of park experiences.

Regularly scheduled summer tours of the underground world, led by a park naturalist, allow visitors to see both the limestone layers of the Dubuque Formation and the pitted dolomite of the Galena Formation. Along the way, it is possible to see the erosional work of subterranean streams and the delicate deposits formed by ground water. There are stalactites and stalagmites, as well as ribbons of flowstone. Several underground pools create an eerie, reflective water environment in the otherwise dry cave.

Above ground, spring wildflowers brighten the leafless forest in April and summer flowers add color to the dark green woods. Song sparrows, orioles, American redstarts, and indigo buntings sing from the branches, but the summer foliage is so dense that it almost seems that the leaves are doing the singing.

The sound of the cold water stream that flows through the valley is soft and constant, broken only by the harsh calls of green-backed herons and kingfishers. From the bridge, visitors can observe trout suspended in the current. Facing upstream, they appear stationary, almost fixed in time like the bridge itself.

The plaque on the old steel bridge reads, "By Gillette—Herzog Mfg.—1899." Steel filigree adorns each end. The structure is still in use, spanning two centuries. On the one side of the bridge the park offers a complex of campgrounds, picnic areas, and a nature-oriented setting. Walking across the bridge, visitors seem to step back into the 1850s.

In 1853, Felix Meighen and his friend Robert Foster built a log cabin store that served the early settlers and the Native Americans. They traded merchandise for venison and animal skins. In 1856, the present building was constructed. For years it was the only store in Fillmore County. Horses tied up to the hitching post, people relaxed in the shade of the white oaks and ash trees. A stagecoach came to town regularly. The yellow clapboard house and red brick store, which closed in 1910, have been carefully restored and preserved by the Minnesota Historical Society.

Today's travelers can still enjoy the coolness of the shade trees and the river valley. The park is an inviting destination, and to take full advantage of the variety of opportunities available, plan an extended stay or repeated visits.

For more information about this park contact: Forestville/Mystery Cave State Park, Route 2, Box 128, Preston, MN 55965. Phone 507–352–5111. See also the address for the DNR Information Center at the front of the book.

Michigan Lily (Lilium michiganense) (Joe Niznik)

Straddle Gallery, Mystery Cave, Forestville State Park (Mark White/Minnesota DNR)

Historic Meighen Store (Bob Firth)

FORT RIDGELY

There is a pastoral innocence about Fort Ridgely as golfers play on the tree-lined fairway. Nine holes surround the ruins of the old fort and wind through the ravines where Dakota warriors charged the garrison in 1862. In this juxtaposition of modern recreation and military history, the park offers picnic grounds, a volleyball court, and a ball diamond situated between a cemetery and the ruins.

In the park's picnic area, two shelters are available for reservations, and two campgrounds are beside a spring-fed creek. Fort Ridgely State Park has a good network of horseback riding, hiking, snowmobile, and ski trails on valley slopes, a backpack campsite, and two lookouts that offer views of the Minnesota River valley. An amphitheater is used in the summer for an annual historic festival and other theatrical presentations. In the winter, part of the golf course is a popular sliding area.

The first purchase of land for the park was made in 1896 as a war memorial. The fort was originally constructed in 1853 on the southeast corner of the Dakota reservation and was built without walls. No one expected trouble. But the Dakota Indians were being forced to live in the same way as the European and American settlers lived at the whim of government agents. A poor crop, racist agents, and a very late annuity payment set up explosive forces that were ignited in 1862.

The significance of the U.S.–Dakota Conflict of 1862 has not been recognized because of the Civil War, and the pivotal role of Fort Ridgely is often understated. The fort's remains, a visitor center, the trails, and interpretive signs make an exciting, enlightening history lesson.

Commissary foundation, Fort Ridgely State Park (Bill Rooks)

For more information about this park contact: Fort Ridgely State Park, Route 1, Box 65, Fairfax, MN 55332. Phone 507–426–7840. See also the address for the DNR Information Center at the front of the book.

FORT SNELLING

For more information about this park contact: Fort Snelling State Park, Highway 5 and Post Road, St. Paul, MN 55111. Phone 612-727-1961. See also the address for the DNR Information Center at the front of the book.

At the confluence of the Minnesota and Mississippi rivers is the historic Pike Island. In 1805, Zebulon Pike met, feasted, and negotiated with the Dakota Indians here. The treaty paved the way for the construction of Fort Snelling in 1821 (the fort was originally called Fort St. Anthony) and gave the U.S. military a strategic position from which it could control two of Minnesota's largest watersheds. The St. Croix River confluence is just downstream, but lacks the cliffs that add to the fort's imposing construction.

The fort, now run by the Minnesota Historical Society, has been reconstructed to give visitors a perspective on the past. The fort becomes a living history theater with interpretation done by a large cast in historic costumes. Cannons explode, stores open for visitors, bread bakes, and there is a buzz of everyday life in the style of the 1820s. A feeling of authenticity complements the careful reconstruction of the walls and buildings by archaeologists and craftsmen. This is a twentieth century structure with a painstaking respect for its nineteenth century predecessor. Other historic sites in the park include the steamboat landing, the old site of Cantonment New Hope, a Dakota internment camp, and Camp Coldwater.

Fort Snelling has the envious distinction of never having been in battle. Instead of bloodshed, the post can brag about many Minnesota firsts—a school, a brass band, a Protestant church, a hospital, and a lending library. Instead of breastworks, the military harnessed St. Anthony Falls for a sawmill and gristmill.

The restored fort, with its round tower, hexagonal tower, pentagonal tower, and semicircular battery, rises from the sedimentary cliff face like a natural outgrowth of limestone. The fort looks down on an equally complex park unit.

Today, the Twin Cities and suburbs surround this fort, and the Mississippi and Minnesota rivers are important for both commerce and recreation. Fort Snelling is flanked by the Minnesota Valley National Wildlife Refuge and Minnehaha Park.

Jet airplanes and barges have replaced ox carts and keelboats, but this is still a hub of transportation. Paved roadways carry the commerce of the Twin Cities across the two rivers and the old fort still watches the passing humanity.

Pike Island features a nature center, which helps people understand the riverine environment of prairie and woodland and the history of the confluence area. Large cottonwood, silver maple, ash, and willow trees grow along the braided channels of the Minnesota. Prairie orchids bloom in the shadow of passing traffic on the freeways.

Most of the park is on the Minnesota River floodplain. There are numerous deer, foxes, woodchucks, and skunks here. The area is also home to one of Minnesota's largest populations of fox snakes. These non-poisonous snakes resemble rattlesnakes and can startle hikers. There are egrets, beavers, minks, muskrats, and waterfowl in the floodplain lakes.

There are numerous picnic sites, a beach, and river and lake fishing for relaxation. Canoeing, hiking, skiing, and biking offer more exercise. The grounds of the state park complex also offer polo grounds. Canoe and boat landings provide access to the rivers and lakes.

A paved bike trail connects with Minnehaha Park and both rivers are designated canoe rivers (watch for barges). Cross-country skiing and snowshoeing are popular in the winter, and unlike many state park visitor centers, this one is open all year. It serves double duty as a warming house in the winter.

Pike Island, Fort Snelling State Park (Joe Niznik)

Pike Island, Minnesota River
(Judy Thompson/Minnesota DNR)

Historic Fort Snelling (Mark Paulson)

HILL ANNEX MINE

This was home to emigrant dreams. The Hill Annex mine supplied the nation's need for iron from 1914 until the latter half of this century. During World War II, the mine produced seven million tons of ore in two years. From Hill Annex's modest beginning to its last shipment in 1979, sixty-three million tons of ore were removed from the earth. Hill Annex began as an underground mine, but switched to open-pit operations after one and a half years.

The visitor center in the park depicts the geologic and historic story of one of the largest open pit mines on Minnesota's Iron Range. Ride the tour bus on the old mine roads, or observe screening plants, mine equipment, and the old cedar-strip watertower. You will go down to the pit that is half full of water and up to the top of Float-rock Hill. Several springs flow into the mine and paint one wall orange. The rock walls are various hues of red with a darker fossil-bearing layer of cretaceous rock, and light-colored glacial overburden.

The pit requires pumping to keep the pit from filling with water. Peregrine falcons have been released on the cliff tops and loons and gulls can be seen on the water.

The park is new, so visitors should watch for additions in the future.

Hill Annex Mine State Park (Daniel J. Cox)

For more information about this park contact: Hill Annex Mine State Park, Box 376, Calumet, MN 55716. Phone 218-247-7215. See also the address for the DNR Information Center at the front of the book.

MILLE LACS KATHIO

Mille Lacs Kathio marks both the outlet of Mille Lacs Lake and the source of the Rum River. The lake was known as "Knife Lake" and the river was called the "Good Spirit River" by the Dakota.

The Kathio National Historic Landmark District is one of only two areas in Minnesota that have been preserved because of their Native American identity. DNR naturalist Jim Cummings called the park "a window in time."

This park has over thirteen archaeological sites which include Archaic, Woodland, and historic cultures. There is an old copper complex with tools produced from copper that was mined near present-day Pine City. The Woodland Period was more sedentary, and pottery that is several hundred years old has been excavated at Woodland sites.

In more modern times, the Dakota encountered the explorers Daniel Greysolon and Sieur du Lhut along the shores of Ogechie and Shakopee lakes near the outlet of Mille Lacs Lake. This was the capitol of the Mdewekanton Dakota people, and they called themselves "Izatys." Poor hand writing combined the *I* and *z* to make a *k* and this error led to the word *Kathio.*

Today visitors can camp, enjoy the seasonal variations from the fire tower, swim and enjoy an extensive trail system with thirty-five miles for hiking and twenty-seven miles for horseback riding. In the winter there is a heated visitor center plus eighteen miles of skiing and nineteen miles of snowshoe trails.

For more information about this park contact: Mille Lacs Kathio State Park, HC-67, Box 85, Onamia, MN 56359. Phone 612-532-3523. See also the address for the DNR Information Center at the front of the book.

Mille Lacs Kathio State Park (Walt Huss)

OLD MILL

The black case steam engine still gets fired up during the summer, and the red-spoked flywheel powers the belt that drives the mill wheels. This is the old mill, a part of Red River valley life in 1896. Nearby is a dove-tailed cabin with a wood-encased well, a split-rail fence, and an outhouse. The inside of the cabin is sparsely furnished and speaks eloquently of the simple life of the early settlers.

This area was homesteaded by Lars Larson Sr. in 1882. He built a water-powered mill in 1886, but that was destroyed by floods in 1888. In 1889, he built a windmill and the wind blew it down. Despite this rash of bad luck, he built another water mill in 1889, north of the park. His son started this steam-powered mill in the same year.

The small steep-walled valley of the Middle River is young and cuts through the same beach that forms the dam at Lake Bronson. The beach and drainage began when glacial Lake Agassiz still existed. The land along the river has always been a corridor for animal life, such as moose, deer, raccoons, and jackrabbits, and most of those species still follow the valley.

Today, visitors are attracted by the mill and the shady river bottom parkland. They are also attracted to the swimming area, the swinging bridge, the picnic grounds, and campgrounds. Kids like the beach and playground and fishing in the old mill pond. There are hiking, snowmobile, and cross-country trails, plus skating and sliding. For birdwatchers, Old Mill can provide surprises because it is a good place for migrants to gather.

For more information about this park contact: Old Mill State Park, Route 1, Box 42, Argyle, MN 56713. Phone 218–437–8174. See also the address for the DNR Information Center at the front of the book.

Historic Larson's Mill, Old Mill State Park
(Carmelita McGurk/Minnesota DNR)

This park marks a continental divide, a place where waters run to the Atlantic Ocean through the Great Lakes and to the Gulf of Mexico through the Mississippi River. It also has a historic corridor that the Dakota and Ojibwe Indians, explorers, and voyageurs used for over two hundred years.

The portage, for which the park is named, was a six-mile carry from the East Savanna River to the West Savanna River, and the trail crossed marsh, swamp, and dense forest. On parts of the trail, travelers had to wade through waist–deep muck and thick mosquitoes, or balance on logs placed end to end. It took five days to get everything across.

Today's visitors can walk the continental divide and hike the Savanna Portage on well-maintained park trails. Several lakes in the park are easier to canoe than the shallow East and West Savanna rivers and offer excellent trout, bass, and panfish fishing. Only electric trolling motors are allowed on park lakes. Motors, boats, and canoes can be rented at the park headquarters.

The park has picnic and camping facilities, miles of hiking, skiing, and snowmobiling trails, a playground and beach at Loon Lake, and back-pack campsites. Exhibits at the park office describe the fur trade.

Much of the park's fifteen thousand acres is wilderness. The forest is primarily northern hardwoods with birch and aspen and some conifers mixed in. There are also extensive leatherleaf-black spruce bogs, and remnant pine stands missed by the early loggers. Animal life in the area includes deer, bears, otters, beavers, and muskrats. Warblers are found in the bogs and loons on the lakes.

Adjacent to the park is the Remote Lake Solitude Area, part of Savanna State Forest. This is an excellent backcountry area for backpackers and skiers.

Savanna Portage State Park (Bob Firth)

For more information about this park contact: Savanna Portage State Park, HCR 3, Box 591, McGregor, MN 55760. Phone 218–426–3271. See also the address for the DNR Information Center at the front of the book.

115

SOUDAN UNDERGROUND MINE

Step back to 1884 when the open pit mine of Captain Elisha Morcom shipped the first ore bound for Two Harbors. Drop down 2,400 feet to a cool fifty-two-degree environment and think about the miners who removed ore from this underground mine from the 1890s to 1962. Soudan is the only underground iron mine that people can go one-half mile underground. It is a unique experience that visitors long remember.

In 1866 miners swept over this ridge in a boom reminiscent of the Californian and Alaskan gold rushes. They were looking for gold in the rocks of Lake Vermilion as they trampled over one of the most valuable ore deposits in Minnesota's history. It wasn't until 1875 that George Stuntz (the park surrounds Stuntz Bay) explored the area and found valuable iron ore.

Eventually, Pennsylvanian Charlemagne Tower was convinced to finance the operation; he proceeded to acquire seventeen thousand acres. A railroad replaced the trails of disheartened gold seekers. Experienced miners from the Upper Peninsula of Michigan, some lumberjacks, and tin miners from Cornwall (called Cousin Jacks) worked with picks and shovels to load the horse-drawn wagons with ore.

The original mine is still visible, but currently underground mining is more unusual in Minnesota. Most of our mines are open pits, but this formation is older and different than that of the Mesabi and Cuyuna ranges. When the open pit walls became too steep, they switched to the underground method. Visitors can park and picnic among red outcroppings in the forest, and walk among mining artifacts near the edge of an open pit before entering a visitor center or taking the mining tour. Above ground visitors can see the dry house, drill shop, crusher house, and engine house. Displays and mine guides help make this story come alive.

The tour goes through an underground world, a land with a new language. Visitors don hard hats and enter a "cage" for the descent into the mine. The mine has a natural airflow below ground; however, water must be pumped out. Grandby cars, "skips," and carbide lamps are part of the mining history. There are the "shaft" and "drifts." "Breasts" are full of ore, and "charging back" means setting the explosives. Wear your jacket: The men who worked here generated a lot of heat from their efforts, but for the visitor, the fifty-degree temperature is very cool. The mine is open during the winter for special group tours.

For those who want a different experience of the park, the Taconite State Trail runs through the park. This long snowmobile and recreational trail traverses six counties and five major population centers.

Several areas in the park have excellent exposures of jaspilite, perhaps Minnesota's most beautiful rock. It's hard to envision that this was the first area of mining dreams in Minnesota.

For more information about this park contact: Soudan Underground Mine State Park, Box 335, Soudan, MN 55782. Phone 218-753-2245. See also the address for the DNR Information Center at the front of the book.

Soudan Underground Mine State Park (Paul Wannarka)

Underground mine exhibit (Greg L. Ryan and Sally A. Beyer)

*Headframe, Soudan Underground Mine State Park
(Carmelita McGurk/Minnesota DNR)*

UPPER SIOUX AGENCY

Upper Sioux Agency State Park preserves both a sense of history and a sample of our natural heritage. The Minnesota Historical Society has restored one of the original residences from the agency (Minnesota's first duplex dwelling), and the Department of Natural Resources has surrounded the duplex with land that captures some of the majesty of the old western territories. This serene setting is a fitting memorial to the victims of the U.S.–Dakota Conflict of 1862 and an appropriate gravesite for Mazomani, a Dakota chief who died trying to make peace.

The wind blows across depressions where homes once stood. The wind also sends waves of energy surging across stands of prairie, just as it did when a warehouse for government allotments stood and a manual labor school offered courses in agriculture, sewing, and carpentry to the Native Americans.

The Yellow Medicine River and its valley is one of the most beautiful in southwestern Minnesota. The deep ravine that the Yellow Medicine River cut is lined with trees, creating a place of solitude. The rippling waters and the birds in the trees make gentle music in this quiet landscape.

The Minnesota River is a slow stream that meanders lazily along, inviting anglers to fish for walleye, bullheads, and catfish. There is a boat access on the river, and scenic views from the ridgetop allow visitors to see the valley and imagine the force of the glacial River Warren that carved the valley.

The Yellow Medicine Interpretive Center helps the curious learn about nature and history (for example, the river is named for the moonseed vine that grows along its banks). There are outstanding horseback riding, skiing, hiking, and snowmobiling trails. In addition, the most popular winter activity is the huge snow sliding hill.

Historic agency site, Upper Sioux Agency State Park (Carmelita McGurk/Minnesota DNR)

For more information about this park contact: Upper Sioux Agency State Park, Route 2, Box 92, Granite Falls, MN 56241. Phone 612–564–4777. See also the address for the DNR Information Center at the front of the book.

ALPHABETICAL LISTING OF STATE PARKS

For more terrific information about Minnesota's state parks, contact the Department of Natural Resources Information Center:

DNR Information Center
500 Lafayette Road
St. Paul, MN 55155–4040
Twin Cities: 296–4776
Toll-free in Minnesota: 800–652–9747 (ask for DNR)
Telecommunications device for deaf: 612–296–5484